LYME DISEASE

THE GREAT IMITATOR

HOW TO PREVENT
AND CURE IT

By Dr. Alvin Silverstein,
Virginia Silverstein, & Robert Silverstein

with a foreword by Leonard H. Sigal, M.D.

AVSTAR Publishing Corp.
P.O. Box 537
Lebanon, NJ 08833

CREDITS

Photos and graphics provided courtesy of:
Centers for Disease Control: pages 16, 32 bot., 47, 74
EcoHealth: pages 18, 20, 35, 43, 84, 94, 105, 108
NIAID, NIH: pages 11, 29, 51, 53, 59, 65, 112
Pfizer Central Research: page 89 (John Stratton): pages 90, 97
Rocky Mountain Laboratories: cover & page 30 (Stanley F. Hayes, Willy
    Burgdorfer, & M. Dan Corwin); page 25 (Dr. Tom Schwan); page 32 top
Robert A. Silverstein: pages 8, 39, 99
Virginia B. Silverstein: page 86
U.S. Bureau of Biological Survey: page 33
Westchester County, NY, Department of Health: pages 114, 116
Wisconsin Department of Natural Resources: page 103

Anecdotal case histories were based on accounts in:
Foderaro, Lisa. W, "For 3 With Lyme Disease, Pain Without End." *New
    York Times,* January 4, 1989, pp. A1, B4. (p. 79)
Justice, Eric, "Housewife Collected Cases, Spurred Recognition in 1975."
    Medical Tribune, November 25, 1987, p. 19. (pp. 13-18)
Schmitz, Anthony, "After the Bite." *Hippocrates,* May/June 1989, pp. 78-84.
    (pp. 13-18)
Seligmann, Jean et al., "Tiny Tick, Big Worry." *Newsweek,* May 2, 1989,
    pp. 66-72. (pp. 50, 58, 97, 98)

The authors and publisher have carefully researched numerous sources to ensure the accuracy and completeness of the information in this book, but we assume no responsibility for any errors or omissions. Any apparent slights against people or organizations mentioned in *Lyme Disease, The Great Imitator,* are unintentional.

The medical information presented in this book is provided for reference only. Consult your doctor for medical advice for specific problems.

Manufactured in the United States of America

Library of Congress Cataloging-in-Publication Data

Silverstein, Alvin.
    Lyme disease, the great imitator : how to prevent and cure it / by Alvin Silverstein, Virginia Silverstein & Robert Silverstein; foreword by Leonard H. Sigal, M.D.
        p.   cm.
    Includes bibliographical references.
    Summary: Discusses the scope and history of this growing health problem, its medical and ecological background, symptoms, diagnosis, treatment, practical methods for avoiding infection, and current research into possible cures.
    ISBN 0-9623653-8-6 : $12.95. — ISBN 0-9623653-9-4 (pbk.) : $5.95
    1. Lyme disease—juvenile literature. (1. Lyme disease.)
I. Silverstein, Virginia B. II. Silverstein, Robert A. III. Title.
RC155.5.S57 1990
616.9'2—dc20 90-81250 CIP AC

For Emily Rachel Silverstein

ACKNOWLEDGMENTS

The authors received invaluable aid from a number of the scientists at the forefront of Lyme disease research, who were extraordinarily generous with their time and knowledge.

Dr. Willy Burgdorfer of the Rocky Mountain Laboratories in Hamilton, Montana, provided important background on his discovery of the Lyme disease spirochete and other aspects of the history of the disease. His encouraging comments about the project were greatly appreciated.

Special thanks to Dr. Leonard H. Sigal, of the Robert Wood Johnson Medical School of the UMDNJ in New Brunswick, New Jersey, for his careful reading of the manuscript, his many fruitful consultations, and the insights he provided into the leading edge of clinical research on Lyme disease.

We are also deeply grateful to Drs. Robert Craven, Bill Letson, and Gayle L. Miller of the Bacterial Zoonoses Branch of the Centers for Disease Control in Fort Collins, Colorado; to Dr. Thomas Mather of the Center for Blood Research in Boston, Massachusetts; to Dr. Andrew Spielman of the Harvard School of Public Health; to Dr. Allen Steere of Tufts University School of Medicine; and to Dr. Raymond Dattwyler of the State University of New York at Stony Brook. They were all kind enough to read the manuscript in detail, and their many helpful comments and suggestions helped to clarify and refine key areas of the subject. The interchange of ideas in conversations with the researchers was enlightening and inspiring.

Thanks also to all those who kindly supplied photographs and information.

ALSO BY THE AUTHORS:

Allergies (Lippincott, 1977)
The Sugar Disease: Diabetes (Lippincott, 1980)
Mice: All About Them (Lippincott, 1980)
FutureLife: The Biotechnology Revolution (Prentice-Hall, 1982)
Headaches: All About Them (Lippincott, 1984)
Heart Disease: America's #1 Killer (Lippincott, 1985)
World of the Brain (Morrow, 1986)
AIDS: Deadly Threat (Enslow, 1986)
Cancer: Can It Be Stopped? (Lippincott, 1987)
Wonders of Speech (Morrow, 1988)
Learning About AIDS (Enslow, 1989)
Genes, Medicine, and You (Enslow, 1989)
John, Your Name Is Famous (AVSTAR, 1989)
Overcoming Acne (Morrow, 1990)

FOREWORD

Lyme disease is an ailment with a short history in the United States, although some of the skin manifestations were first described in Europe over a century ago. It was only fifteen years ago that Lyme disease was first described by Allen C. Steere and his coworkers. It has been less than ten years since *Borrelia burgdorferi* was identified as the cause of the disease and specific diagnostic tests were developed for Lyme disease. The first studies of oral antibiotic therapy for Lyme disease were performed at Yale in the late 1970s. By 1990, a number of drugs and formulations have been tested and found effective in the disease. Much has been learned in a very short time, although there are still many things to be learned.

It is now time to look at all that is known, not only to educate the public but also to combat the second epidemic in our midst, that of Lyme hysteria. Half-truths and speculations have found their way into the body of conventional wisdom and have led to unnecessary anxiety and even desperation on the part of patients and the parents of the children with Lyme disease. Unsupported statements have been made which minimize the confidence of patients in testing and therapy. This is happening at the very time when both are improving, due to advancements in technology and physicians' skills. The purpose of this volume is the following: to allay fear and to educate.

The past history of Lyme disease consists of a series of investigative triumphs. This series of successes starts with Polly Murray and Drs. Steere and Burgdorfer in the 1970s. It extends to the many researchers, around the world and across the United States, who are currently exploring the molecular biology of *Borrelia burgdorferi* and investigating the nature of the immune response to the organism, new more sensitive and specific diagnostic tests, and new more effective therapies. There is every reason to believe that our grasp of the disease and our skills in diagnosing and treating the disease will improve beyond the current, not inconsiderable, levels of understanding. There is no reason for hysteria, although there is reason for concern. There is no reason for fear, although there is reason for attention.

Leonard H. Sigal, M.D.
Assistant Professor
Department of Medicine and Department
of Molecular Genetics and Microbiology
Director, Lyme Disease Center
Robert Wood Johnson Medical School of
the University of Medicine and Dentistry
of New Jersey
New Brunswick, New Jersey

CONTENTS

1.
A NEW DISEASE THREAT

A new disease has been worrying Americans for the past few years—especially in the summertime. It's called Lyme disease, and each spring scary articles about it begin to appear in newspapers and popular magazines. As the days grow warmer, special Lyme disease clinics are flooded with phone calls, and labs are swamped with blood samples to be tested for the disease. Summer is the season for picnics and camping trips, but across the country people are afraid to go out in the woods or fields. Some parents won't even let their children play in their own backyards, for fear they'll catch Lyme disease.

In some areas Lyme disease seems to be the main thing people talk about in the summertime. Luke Pittoni, copresident of Stamford, Connecticut's parent-teacher council declares, "People are petrified of it. It's almost a panic situation."

"We are in the midst of two epidemics," says Dr. Leonard Sigal, director of the Lyme Disease Center at the Robert Wood Johnson Medical School in New Brunswick, New Jersey, "—Lyme disease and Lyme disease hysteria."

And yet, there are effective treatments for Lyme disease, as well as ways of preventing it.

A Growing Danger

Our "new" epidemic isn't really all that new. Doctors in the

United States have known about Lyme disease since 1975. European doctors were already familiar with it—reports of European cases dated back to 1909. In the 1970s Lyme disease seemed to be a rather rare condition. Then, in the late 1980s, it began to attract nationwide attention on TV, in newspapers and magazines. Suddenly almost everyone had heard something about this previously "unknown" disease.

Because of the attention, many undiagnosed cases of Lyme disease were discovered. But at the same time, tens of thousands of people worriedly rushed to their doctors demanding blood tests. At one lab, which tested 35,000 blood samples for Lyme disease in 1988, for example, only 1 percent tested positive. Many doctors and health experts feel that Lyme disease dangers are being greatly exaggerated by the media.

The danger is growing, though. Cases of Lyme disease have been reported in at least forty-three states in the U.S. and on six continents worldwide. It strikes people of all ages, and according to some estimates there may be as many as ten thousand new cases each year—most of them undiagnosed. Some experts are beginning to call the problem an epidemic.

The Great Imitator

Lyme disease can produce a puzzling variety of symptoms, often resembling those of other ailments. A victim may suffer from flu-like headaches, fatigue, chills, aches and pains. Stiffness in the joints may develop; crippling arthritis may occur. In most cases the symptoms gradually go away, but sometimes the disease can lead to such serious complications as nerve damage and heart problems. This great variety of symptoms can make Lyme disease rather hard to diagnose, and it was one of the reasons medical experts took so long to discover it. Now doctors have begun to refer to Lyme disease as the "great imitator," or "great masquerader," because its symptoms can mimic those of so many other diseases.

Even after Lyme disease was recognized as a new kind of illness, it took a number of years for medical researchers to figure out what caused it. Eventually it was discovered that this is a bacterial disease, spread by the bites of a very tiny tick. It is called the deer tick because the adult tick normally lives on deer, but it can also feed on field mice, raccoons, birds, household pets, or humans. (It is much smaller than the common dog tick.) Rocky Mountain spotted fever was once the most common disease spread by ticks; in 1984 it was passed by Lyme disease, which has been the number one tick-borne disease since then.

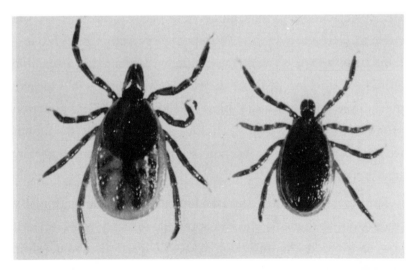

A highly magnified view of adult deer ticks. A female is on the left, and a male on the right.

Stopping the Epidemic

Lyme disease can be cured. A number of drugs are effective against it, and it can be treated in any stage, but it is best treated as early as possible. A problem, though, is that the disease isn't always easy to diagnose. Blood tests often don't detect the bacterium until weeks after the person was bitten by a tick. Indeed, the person may not even be aware of having been bitten, because the deer ticks are so tiny. Although many people develop a typical "bull's-eye"-shaped rash around the bite, not everyone does.

Doctors don't have a vaccination against Lyme disease, yet. But there are things you can do to avoid catching it, even though ticks carrying it might be lurking in the grass in your backyard.

Government health agencies are working with state and local authorities to help make people more aware of Lyme disease. Dr. Patrick Moore of the Centers for Disease Control (CDC) in Atlanta, Georgia, which is swamped every summer with questions from people all over the country, recommends a sensible attitude toward the possible dangers. "We want people to take precautions to prevent tick bites and to seek medical attention promptly if they develop suspicious symptoms," he says, "but we don't want people to become so overly concerned that they stay indoors."

The surest protection against Lyme disease is prevention. By finding out as much as you can about the disease, you can learn how to avoid it. In this book you will learn all about Lyme disease—what it is, how people catch it, how to avoid catching it, and what to do if you think you might have it.

2.
DISCOVERING
A "NEW" DISEASE

For years Polly Murray was told by doctors that her headaches, fatigue, rashes, fevers, and stiff and swollen joints were nothing to worry about. They implied that she was exaggerating her problems, and perhaps they had no real physical cause. The doctors told Mrs. Murray to take up some hobbies to keep her mind off these "psychosomatic symptoms." In the mid-1970s, though, the rest of her family began to experience odd symptoms as well.

"In the summer of 1975, it really was bad," she says. Her husband had to walk on crutches because his knees were stiff and swollen, and he developed a rash on his back. Her daughter's tongue swelled, and her eldest son's face suddenly became paralyzed, then returned to normal after a while. Her other two sons suffered from headaches and badly inflamed knees, and one had such a stiff neck that he couldn't turn his head. Even the family pets were ill.

Looking for Answers

The frightened mother knew something was going on. She wondered if there might be some poison in the air or water, or if there had been a radiation leak from nearby nuclear power plants. But when she had the family's drinking water tested, it was fine.

That summer, doctors came up with a diagnosis for one of the

Murray boys—they said he was suffering from juvenile rheumatoid arthritis (JRA). The symptoms seemed to match, but JRA is not a very common disease.

Polly Murray started calling other parents in the Lyme, Connecticut area where she lived and found out that eighteen others in the area suffered from similar complaints. This seemed like a very strange coincidence to her. She brought her findings around to local doctors. "I kept saying, look, the rash is common, then you get the joint problems; there was a pattern to the whole thing." But they assured her there wasn't any disease that fit her description. One doctor did suggest she contact the Connecticut State Health Department; she did, in October of 1975.

The Disease Detective

The Health Department had received a similar complaint from another concerned parent, Judith Mensch. Her child had been diagnosed with JRA, and she knew of four others with the same diagnosis—all in the same small Connecticut area. The state health officials called in a rheumatology expert, Dr. Allen Steere at the Yale University Division of Rheumatology, who had just completed training with the epidemic intelligence service of the U.S. Centers for Disease Control. By the time he interviewed Mrs. Murray, she had collected thirty-five case histories of the "mysterious arthritis" in Lyme and the surrounding communities of Old Lyme and East Haddam.

Dr. Steere was fascinated. Arthritis was not supposed to be a contagious disease, but clusters of cases like this suggested that people might somehow be "catching" arthritis. Dr. Steere, now chief of the division of rheumatology at Tufts-New England Medical School in Boston, believed that some types of arthritis were infectious. He didn't think there would ever be an opportunity to prove his theory "since an outbreak of arthritis is a very unusual event," but, just four months after he began a post-doctoral fellowship at Yale, this unusual event had occurred.

By May 1976 Dr. Steere and his colleagues had found thirty-nine children and twelve adults in and around Lyme, Connecticut who were apparently suffering from a similar form of arthritis.

Normally JRA affects about one out of each 100,000 children. And yet, in a total population of 12,000, Dr. Steere had turned up thirty-nine JRA cases. In one area, half of the children affected lived on only four roads, with an occurrence 10,000 times the normal rate! Obviously what was happening in this Connecticut community was not ordinary juvenile rheumatoid arthritis. That summer Dr. Steere and his colleagues announced the discovery of "Lyme arthritis," named for the town. The name was later changed to *Lyme disease* because many other medical problems are associated with it.

Tracing the Cause

Dr. Steere and his colleagues observed that Lyme disease did not seem to be very contagious, compared to an illness like a cold or the flu, for example. Often only one member of a family came down with its symptoms. When more than one family member was affected, sometimes a year or more went by between one case and another.

There were some other suggestive patterns, too. Most of the victims first noticed symptoms during the summer months. A

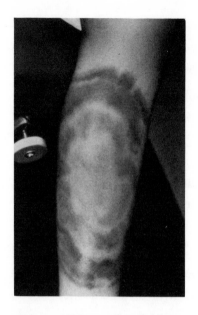

Erythema chronicum migrans,
the bull's-eye rash
often seen in the early
stage of Lyme disease.

quarter of them also described a characteristic rash that appeared before the arthritis set in. It started out as a little red bump and then spread to form a reddened bull's-eye rash as much as 20 inches across. That sounded to the researchers like the bite of an insect or an arachnid (a group that includes spiders and ticks). The warm summer months would be the time when such creatures are most likely to be active. The fact that the outbreak occurred in a rural location, with the largest numbers of cases in heavily wooded areas, provided further support for the theory. The rash typically occurred on the chest, abdomen, back, and buttocks, in places where a crawling insect or arachnid might have been stopped by clothing. This suggested to the researchers that the carrier of the disease was probably not a flying insect, like a mosquito.

In addition to examining and questioning all the people in the Lyme area who had developed the mysterious arthritis, Dr. Steere searched through the medical literature to see if anything like it had occurred before. He discovered some old reports of a similar situation that occurred in Europe, back in 1909. Arvid Afzelius, a Swedish physician, described an expanding red rash that developed in patients who were bitten by the sheep tick, *Ixodes ricinus*. He called the condition erythema migrans ("migrating red rash"), later changed to erythema chronicum migrans (ECM) by Dr. B. Lipschutz.

In later outbreaks, European physicians were successful in treating ECM rashes with penicillin. They concluded that the disease was caused by a bacterium and not a virus, since antibiotics don't work against viral infections. Dr. Steere thought the ECM rash sounded very similar to the bull's-eye rash of some of the Lyme arthritis patients, although the European patients did not develop arthritis.

But only one of the Lyme disease patients remembered being bitten by a tick, and when the researchers tested fluid from their joints for 38 tick-transmitted diseases and 178 other diseases carried by arthropods, not one of the tests was positive!

The Lyme Disease Tick

The following summer, in 1977, Dr. Steere found nine patients who remembered being bitten by ticks, and one of them saved the tick for the researcher. Dr. Steere brought the tiny pinhead-sized tick to his colleagues and found that it was a northern deer tick of the genus *Ixodes*. (It is called a deer tick because it feeds on deer in its adult stage.) Tests revealed that on the Lyme side of the Connecticut river, the deer tick was twelve times more common than on the other shore where the disease had not spread.

The particular tick species that carries Lyme disease was

not identified until 1979. The delay is understandable. The deer tick is very tiny, and there are more than 250 different species of *Ixodes* ticks around the world—all rather similar looking. These ticks also have similar life cycles, but they don't interbreed and are separate species.

Andrew Spielman, at the Harvard School of Public Health, was the first to identify the Lyme disease tick as *Ixodes dammini*, a species closely related to the European disease-carrying sheep tick, *I. ricinus*.

Dr. Spielman and his colleagues had first discovered this species while they were studying another tick-carried disease called babesiosis, which has malaria-like symptoms. Researchers originally believed that the tick that carried babesiosis was *Ixodes scapularis*, a species that was thought to live along the eastern coast from Florida to New England. But the northern tick turned out to be a different species, and a new name had

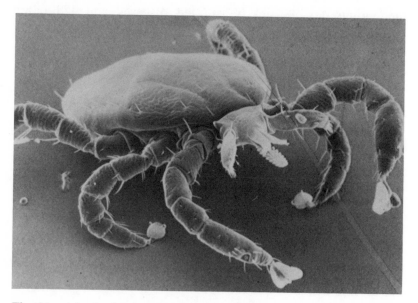

The deer tick, *Ixodes dammini*, greatly magnified.

to be given to it. *I. dammini* was chosen in honor of Dr. Gustave Dammin, also at Harvard.

Although 80 percent of the Lyme disease cases are caused by this northern deer tick, *I. dammini*, other ticks can also spread the ailment. *I. ricinus* and *I. persulcatus* carry the disease in Europe and Asia, *I. scapularis* and *Amblyoma americanum* (the Lone Star tick) in the southeastern United States, and *I. pacificus* in the western states.

Another Part of the Puzzle

Ticks do not actually cause Lyme disease; they carry the microorganism responsible for the symptoms and transmit it when they drink the blood of a mouse or deer—or a human. When the researchers had identified the tick carrier, they still didn't know what kind of microorganism was causing the disease. There was evidence that it was a bacterium, but none of the tests of Lyme patients had found it.

Several more years passed before the real culprit in Lyme disease—the bacterium—was discovered.

Dr. Willy Burgdorfer, an international authority on tick-borne diseases working at the Rocky Mountain Laboratories in Hamilton, Montana, and Dr. Jorge Benach of the New York State Health Department had been studying Rocky Mountain spotted fever on Long Island, where a number of fatal cases had occurred. They thought at first that dog ticks (*Dermacentor variabilis*) were carrying the microbe that causes the disease (a rickettsia), but tests showed that they were not. Next the researchers decided to check another common tick in the area—the deer tick. Again the tests failed to show the spotted fever rickettsia.

In the fall of 1981, Dr. Benach collected a new batch of

deer ticks on Shelter Island, off the eastern Long Island coast. Tests at Dr. Burgdorfer's laboratory found no rickettsias, but microscopic studies showed that corkscrew-shaped spirochete bacteria were swarming in the gut of each tick. Remembering some early European reports linking spirochetes with ECM, Dr. Burgdorfer tested serum samples from Lyme disease patients for antibodies against the spirochetes. The tests were positive. A colleague, Dr. Alan G. Barbour, isolated the spirochetes and worked out ways to grow them in the lab.

Once Dr. Burgdorfer had identified the bacteria responsible for the disease, other researchers began to confirm his findings. University of Minnesota Medical School researchers studied the organism's DNA and determined it was a new species of bacteria of the genus *Borrelia*. In 1984 they named it *Borrelia burgdorferi* after its discoverer.

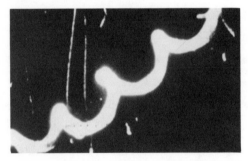

Borrelia burgdorferi,
the Lyme disease
spirochete.

B. burgdorferi is suprisingly similar to another spirochete —the one that causes syphilis. The two microbes produce many similar symptoms, although the Lyme bacterium is not transmitted sexually. Like most spirochetes, *B. burgdorferi* is small and difficult to detect. It passes through many filters designed to hold back bacteria, which is why it had taken so long to find it.

Once the organism was isolated it was easy to track down the animals it was found in. Edward M. Bosler of the New York State

Department of Health found the spirochete in all stages of *I. dammini*, as well as in mice, voles, and deer. In field studies on Shelter Island, up to 90 percent of *I. dammini* were found to be infected with *B. burgdorferi*, compared to the usual 20-40 percent in the northeast.

Why Is It Spreading Now?

The mystery of what causes Lyme disease has been solved. But another mystery still remains. Researchers are still puzzled about why this relatively rare disease became epidemic in Connecticut in the 1970s, and why it is now rapidly spreading across the country when it had been around for more than a century.

The spread of Lyme disease seems to be following a similar expansion of the tick that carries it. The northern deer tick was described at least as far back as the 1920s on Naushon Island in Massachusetts (where deer have been plentiful even at times when they were scarce elsewhere in New England), but nowhere else. In the 1960s *I. dammini* was found at more sites along the New England coast. By the 1980s the tick was found from New Hampshire to Virginia, as well as inland in Pennsylvania and Maryland.

Why is the range of the tick spreading? Was the spirochete always present in the ticks? If so why didn't it infect people before? Is it a new mutation from another, "harmless" bacterium? Or did *Borrelia burgdorferi* only recently come to America?

Some European researchers are annoyed that the disease is now called Lyme disease. They claim this is a European disease that may actually have been around for centuries. European researchers had linked the disease to many of the known symptoms, such as meningitis, decades before the disease was

21

"discovered" in Lyme, Connecticut.

In Europe the sheep tick, *Ixodes ricinus*, is the carrier of the disease, and researchers have identified two strains of *Borrelia burgdorferi*: one found mainly in central Europe (Austria, Germany, and Switzerland) and another found mostly in Scandinavian countries. European researchers have noticed a surge in cases of the disease in recent years, just as in the United States.

Some researchers believe that the disease may have come to America fairly recently. It has been suggested that migrating birds may have carried infected ticks from Europe to American shores. But Dr. Jorge Benach, at the New York State Health Department, points out that migrating birds tend to fly "north-south, rather than east-west." He believes infected ticks crossed the oceans aboard ships in the fur of domestic animals, such as sheep, or on stowaway rats or mice.

Researchers are still exploring the possibilities of how and when Lyme disease first started, but one thing is certain—it is a spreading global problem.

***

As for the original case in Lyme: The Murray family's ailments were cured with antibiotics. Twice Polly Murray has been reinfected with the disease. "Living in the area, you're liable to be rebitten," she says. She has given lectures about how to detect the disease early, and "how patients can sometimes affect the course of research by following their hunches." She is also actively fighting for more funds for Lyme disease research, and for increasing the awareness of doctors and the public about the disease.

3.
A GROWING PROBLEM

It wasn't very long after Lyme disease was discovered in Connecticut that the number of cases began to increase dramatically. By 1980 the problem was considered serious enough for the U.S. Centers for Disease Control (CDC) to begin monitoring the number and location of cases across the nation. In 1982 there were 491 new reported cases. By 1985 the number of new cases tripled to 1520, and the 1988 total of 4572 was more than nine times the 1982 amount. CDC researchers believe the 1989 total was over 7000 new cases. In the nine-year span from 1980 to 1989, more than 21,000 cases were reported to the CDC.

However, as Dr. Paul LaVoie, a Lyme disease expert in San Francisco, points out, "the reported cases are just the tip of the iceberg."

"We all assume that Lyme is under-reported," commented Dr. Ted Tsai at the Centers for Disease Control. There are no federal regulations requiring doctors to report incidents of Lyme disease. Many cases are not included in the count because they don't fit into the official definition. (Not everyone who has the disease shows all the specific symptoms and conditions spelled out in this definition.) The laboratory tests are not always accurate and may miss a substantial fraction of the actual cases. For these and other reasons, many experts believe the true number of cases may be four to ten times higher than the reported totals.

Why Are the Lyme Statistics Going Up?

Some experts claim that the actual numbers of cases of Lyme disease are not really going up as fast as they seem to be; most of the increase in Lyme disease cases, they say, is due to a growing awareness of the disease among physicians and the general public. Cases that would not have been recognized just a few years ago are now being diagnosed.

Health officials also believe that weather patterns may have contributed to the recent trend. Winters were milder than usual during the eighties, and the warmer temperatures allowed more ticks to survive—thus increasing the chances for infected ticks to infect humans.

The steady expansion of America's suburbs has also contributed to explosive increases in the tick populations. As homesites are carved out of woodlands, some of the wild animal species have been forced out, but mice and deer are thriving. They have been multiplying and living closer to humans—and bringing their ticks along with them.

Whatever the reasons for the increasing numbers, most experts now agree with Dr. Willy Burgdorfer at Rocky Mountain Laboratories that "We're definitely seeing a spread of the disease in many states."

When the CDC began monitoring Lyme cases in 1980, there were reports from only eleven states, all concentrated in the northeast and midwest. Now Lyme disease reports come in from at least forty-three states, coast to coast, as well as every continent in the world, except Antarctica.

Experts believe that the numbers of ticks that carry the disease are greatly increasing, as their range of habitation is expanding. In Westchester County, New York, for example, the

Ixodes tick is a very serious problem. Dr. Allen Steere, a pioneer Lyme disease researcher, points out that when he "began working on this in 1975, the disease was really confined to the southeast corner of Connecticut. It's clear that it's moved into a lot of areas where it was not at an earlier time, including Westchester county, where the first case I know of was in 1978. Now it's just one house after another that has someone with the disease." Recently, researchers found an average of 1½ ticks per square yard in their test areas in Westchester county!

Although Lyme disease has been reported in most states, most of the cases are still clustered in three areas—in the northeast, the upper midwest, and along the Pacific coast. In

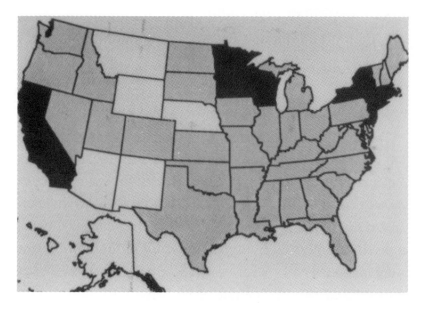

Lyme disease cases have been reported in 43 of the 50 states in the U.S. Black areas indicate regions with the highest Lyme disease rates.

fact, 95 percent of the cases have occurred in just nine states, all in these regions: California, Connecticut, Massachusetts, Minnesota, New Jersey, New York, Pennsylvania, Rhode Island, and Wisconsin. About 80 percent of the cases were reported in the six northeastern states; two New York counties (Westchester and Suffolk) account for more than 40 percent of all the Lyme disease cases in the nation.

However, federal health officials point out that the disease is spilling over into new areas—Pennsylvania and Maryland, for example, as well as Illinois and Iowa. In Texas no cases were reported when the CDC began monitoring the disease; now more than fifty are reported each year, and some officials believe the actual numbers are much higher.

A Lyme Disease Epidemic?

Lyme disease is now the number one vector-borne disease (a disease carried by an animal or insect) in the United States. In some areas it has already become an epidemic, and health officials are worried about how large the numbers may grow.

The epidemic can expand rapidly in communities where there are many deer, once the disease moves into the area. In one small coastal community in Massachusetts, for example, Lyme disease was quite rare before 1980. Then disease-carrying ticks spread from a nearby nature preserve into the community. Within a seven-year period, more than one-third of the 190 residents were infected with Lyme disease. Those who lived closest to the preserve had an infection rate of 66 percent!

Although people who live near woods have the highest infection rates, "You can get this disease in your backyard. You don't have to go wandering into the woods," says Dr. Anita Curran, former health commissioner of Westchester County, New York. In fact, Edward Bosler, disease control specialist with the New York State Health Department, says that "72-77 percent of patients acquired Lyme on their own property or near their homes."

Ticks are finding new suburban home developments an ideal place to breed. "Even if you spray your back yard and kill all the ticks on your property, they will spill over from neighbors' yards," says Dr. Joan Budd, senior public health physician at the New Jersey Department of Health.

In southeastern New York state, where Lyme disease is firmly established, a study found that those who worked outdoors were nearly six times more likely to have antibodies for the disease than the average person in the area. Children in the area got the disease more than adults, because they typically spent more time outside. Pet owners whose pets were allowed out of doors also had a higher rate of infection.

Many people, especially those in high-risk areas, are quite frightened about Lyme disease. Some go to great extremes to avoid the outdoors during the spring and summer months. Others take comfort from the fact that Lyme disease is curable in nearly every stage, when properly diagnosed. Instead of limiting their lives, they merely take some extra precautions as they continue to enjoy the outdoors.

4.
THE TICK
AND ITS WORLD

Most people tend to think of all the small, crawly creatures as "bugs" or insects, and ticks seem to fit into that category, too. Actually, though, ticks are not insects. Instead, they are more closely related to spiders. In fact, the scientific name for the group to which both ticks and spiders belong, *arachnids*, comes from a Greek word meaning "spider." Like spiders, ticks have eight legs, rather than the six that are found on insects.

Ticks are parasites. They live by feeding on other animals. Instead of killing their prey, as the hunters of the animal world do, ticks merely hitch a ride for a while on a suitable animal host. While they are living as uninvited guests, the ticks feed by sucking their host's blood. Humans are not the ideal hosts for any of the varied kinds of ticks in the world, but many of them will bite a human if conditions are right.

Ixodes dammini, the tick that causes Lyme disease in the northeastern and midwestern United States, feeds on white-tailed deer during part of its life cycle. That is why it is called the deer tick. But it might better have been called the mouse tick, as we shall see later. Dogs, cats, horses, and cattle also are among the unlucky hosts for this tick. In fact, scientists have already found forty-nine species of birds and twenty-nine species of mammals that can serve as hosts for *Ixodes* ticks.

Ticks may carry parasites of their own: bacteria, viruses, and other microorganisms. When a tick bites an animal it may transmit these microbes to its host. Rocky Mountain spotted fever is spread in this way by the American dog tick. This disease causes about thirty human deaths each year in the United States. Other tick-borne diseases are Q fever, tularemia, Texas cattle fever, relapsing fever, Colorado tick fever, and Lyme disease.

Portrait of a Tick

A number of species of *Ixodes* ticks are carriers of Lyme disease in various parts of the world. But wherever they are found, these ixodids look pretty much alike. They are rather small, for ticks. The immature ones, called nymphs, are about 1-2 mm long—little larger than the period at the end of this sentence, or just about the size of a poppy seed. They are a brownish black in color, but when they are feeding their bodies swell up to triple their original size and become more grayish.

The deer tick: nymph, adult male, and adult female.

29

An adult deer tick is about the size of a sesame seed (3 mm for a female, 2.5 mm for a male). The adult female is a brick red color, with a black shield on her back. (After feeding, she turns blue-black and may swell up to the size of a pea.) The adult male is all black and somewhat smaller than the female.

Under a magnifying glass, you can see that a tick has a large, rather flattened body, and a very small head. A powerful microscope reveals more details.

The tick's four pairs of legs are many-jointed, and each ends in a claw. The tips of the legs also carry adhesive pads, which help the tick to cling to its host.

The mouthparts on the front of the tick's head are perfectly adapted to its way of life. Two palps ("feelers") serve as sense organs. They are covered with hairs and other sensitive structures that help the tick to find a host. Between the two palps is a very specialized mouth, the hypostome. It is long and slim and covered with barbs, like the barbs on a fish hook.

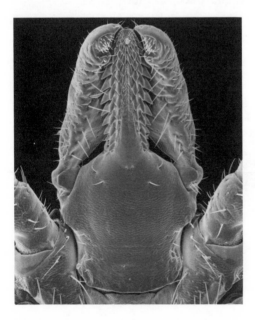

The tick's mouthparts. Notice the barbs on the long hypostome in the center.

The tick uses its hypostome to drill a hole in the host's skin until its tip enters a tiny blood vessel. Then the barbs help to hold the tick in place while it sucks up blood—like drinking through a straw.

Life Cycle of the Deer Tick

The life story of a human spans a period of perhaps seventy or eighty years. The first quarter or so is a time of growing and maturing, from a helpless baby to an adult man or woman, capable of starting off a new generation. Bearing and raising children may occupy twenty or thirty years of the middle part of a human life, and then there is a very long and gradual aging.

The life story of a deer tick is very different. It is much shorter—only two years from start to finish. The tick begins life as a tiny egg and passes through several stages on its way to adulthood. At each stage it looks rather unlike its former self, and it behaves differently, too. Mama and papa tick don't have to cope with a "midlife crisis" or worry about how to occupy themselves after the children have grown up and left home. Once they have provided for the new generation, their life is over.

Strictly speaking, a deer tick's life starts in the fall, when an adult male and female mate. Specialized sex cells, the male's sperm and the female's eggs, join to produce new individuals. The male dies soon afterward, but the mother tick, still carrying the developing eggs inside her body, survives through the cold of winter.

In the spring she lays her eggs among the fallen leaves and other debris covering the ground of the forest. After a month

31

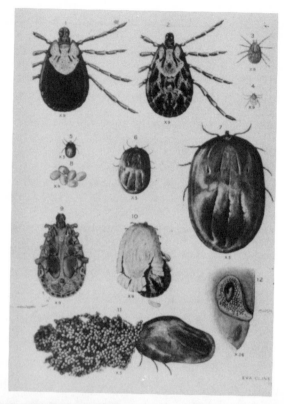

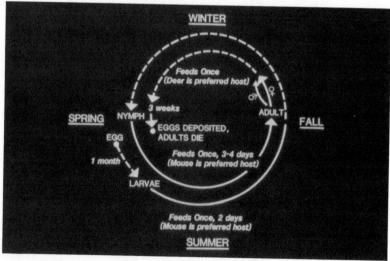

Life cycle of the deer tick, *Ixodes dammini.*

or so, during the early summer, tiny larvae hatch out. The larva is the first stage of the tick's active life. It has six legs, rather than the eight it will have as an adult, and it is barely visible. Ravenously hungry, the tick larva seeks out a host. It cannot jump or fly; it can only crawl—and it is so small that it can't crawl very fast or far. So its most likely host will be some small warm-blooded animal—most likely a mouse. Clinging to the host, the larva sucks up its first blood meal.

In many parts of the country the white-footed mouse is the animal most heavily infested with *Ixodes* larvae. The larvae feed for about two days, then drop off and find a place to rest. That single blood meal is enough to last them until the following spring. They remain hidden away in some cozy safe spot through the rest of the summer, the fall, and the winter. From the outside, nothing seems to be happening. But inside the tick larva's body complicated changes are taking place.

The following spring, the tick is ready to present its new self to the world. It sheds its outer covering (which is more like a tough, light-weight suit of armor than the skin we humans have) to reveal a longer, more ticklike body, more developed

The white-footed mouse, main host of the tick larva and nymph.

mouthparts, and eight legs in place of the six it had. It still is not an adult, though. The tick is now in a sort of "adolescent," middle stage, called a nymph.

After all those changes, the young tick has used up its store of food from the larval blood meal. Now it is hungry again, and it searches for a host. Again, the most likely host will be a white-footed mouse, but the nymph is not particular. If some other animal—a raccoon, a dog or cat, or even a human—happens to pass by, the nymph will hitch a ride and settle down for a feast. During this second meal of its life, the tick nymph continues to suck for about four days, and its elastic abdomen swells greatly as the blood store grows. Usually the nymph feeds some time in May, June, or July, but if it has not found a suitable host by then it can take its meal later—in August or even the early fall.

After feeding, the nymph drops off its animal host and crawls away to some quiet place to rest. Now another major change occurs. The nymph's body is remodeled, using the blood from its meal as fuel and building materials, and then it molts (sheds its outer covering) once more. At last it is an adult.

The adult tick's body will not change any more, but it is hungry again. This time it needs refueling for a different purpose—to form the sex cells that will produce the next generation. The adult tick crawls up a blade of grass or some other vegetation and waits for an animal to pass by.

Scientists are still studying how the tick finds its host. It has no eyes or ears, but its sensory palps can pick up very tiny differences in temperature. They are also sensitive to various chemicals such as the carbon dioxide in exhaled air. So body warmth, breath, and perhaps some body scents may help to

The white-
tailed deer.

alert the tick that a warm-blooded animal is nearby. It may also pick up vibrations produced when a moving animal disturbs the grass or underbrush.

In any event, the tick is ready. Perched on a leaf or twig, it waves its front pair of legs in the air, in a manner that researchers call "questing." When it crawls or drops onto a passing animal, the claws and adhesive pads at the tips of its legs will help it to latch on.

Adult deer ticks can feed on many different hosts. In the northeastern United States they are usually found on white-tailed deer, but other mammals (including humans and their pets) and even birds will do. After grabbing hold, the tick typically crawls about for a while, looking for a juicy spot, then sinks its hypostome into the host's skin.

Male ticks feed only briefly, and their bodies do not swell. Their job is to produce sperm (which are very tiny cells, far too small to see without a microscope) and then to mate. Female

35

ticks need a much bigger blood meal. The eggs that they produce are much larger than sperm cells, and each is equipped with a food supply to support the developing embryo until the egg hatches. The female's blood meal also provides her with the energy for mating, for surviving through the cold winter, and for laying her eggs the following spring.

The adult female remains attached to her host, feeding, for about seven days if she is not disturbed. During this time her body swells hugely, ballooning up to look like a grape. (After a blood meal, some *Ixodes* ticks are more than one hundred times their original weight!) Actually, the tick takes in even more blood that her body could hold. Gradually she concentrates the blood meal, keeping the nutrients and "spitting" the extra fluid back into the host's blood vessel. Microbes from the tick's gut may be transferred to the host with this fluid.

The adult ticks mate while they are still on their host. The males die soon after mating, but the female lives on over the winter to start the cycle again. In the spring a single female deer tick may lay as many as 2,500 eggs!

Spreading the Spirochetes

Tick larvae are nearly always free of spirochetes when they hatch. They may pick up these bacteria during their first blood meal, if their host is already infected. The newly infected larvae cannot pass on the spirochetes to another host until the following year, though, because they do not feed again before they molt into their next form, the nymphal stage.

If a nymph was not infected during its first blood meal, as a larva, it now has another chance to pick up the Lyme disease spirochete, *Borrelia burgdorferi*. It may take in the mircrobe as it feeds on its new host. If it was infected as a larva, it can pass on the spirochete to the host of its nymphal feeding. Since white-footed mice are the favorite hosts for both the larvae and the nymphs of the deer tick, transfers are frequent and keep the bacterium circulating among the mouse population.

The varied feeding habits of *Ixodes* nymphs also make it easy for microbes to pass into other warm-blooded hosts. In fact, the nymph is the form of the deer tick that is responsible for most of the human and pet cases of Lyme disease. Some experts feel that between 70 and 90 percent of people who contract Lyme disease have been bitten by a nymph.

Because the nymph is so small, hardly larger than the period at the end of this sentence, it often is not noticed by its human host, or it might be mistaken for a scab or a speck of dirt. Its bite is usually painless, too. (Most people who come down with Lyme disease do not recall ever having been bitten.) So the chances are high that the tick nymph may be allowed to remain on the skin undisturbed for its full feeding time.

Researchers have found that it usually takes about twenty-four hours for the Lyme disease bacterium to be transmitted by a feeding nymph to its host. Transmission takes longer at the adult stage, about forty-eight hours, but the adults are larger and much more likely to be noticed and removed before they have been feeding that long.

Since the adults are usually active in the fall, many people visit their doctors then, complaining about tick bites. But, for most, the real damage has been done months before, in late May, June, or July when the nymphs were active.

There is some evidence that infected adult ticks feeding on white-tailed deer do not usually transmit *Borrelia burgdorferi* to their host. So the deer do not take an active part in spreading the disease, although they contribute indirectly, by serving as the main hosts that support the adult tick populations.

In some surveys of Northeastern states, scientists have found that one out of every four nymphs and half of all the adult ticks carry the spirochete. Other surveys in more heavily infested areas have shown up to 90 percent of the ticks carrying the *Borrelia* microbe. On the west coast, where the infection rate for Lyme disease is lower than in the northeast or midwest, only a few percent of the *Ixodes* ticks had spirochetes in their guts.

Scientists believe that part of the reason Lyme disease is spreading so rapidly is that so many different animals are capable of carrying, and therefore, spreading *Ixodes* ticks.

In addition to the various mammal and bird hosts, lizards and other reptiles can also be infested by Lyme-disease-carrying ticks. The *Borrelia* spirochete itself, however, is not easily transferred to lizards; so these animals do not play a role in spreading the disease. In fact, in the western U.S. lizards seem to be helping to keep the Lyme disease rates low. The *Borrelia*-carrying ticks in that region, *Ixodes pacificus*, are found mainly on lizards and jackrabbits. The jackrabbits can infect the ticks, but there are many more lizards than jackrabbits around for hungry ticks to find. Researchers have discovered that only 1 to 2 percent of the *Ixodes pacificus* ticks in the west are infected with *Borrelia*.

In spite of the many kinds of animals that can carry ticks and be infected by the *Borrelia* spirochete, the white-footed mouse and the white-tailed deer seem to be the keys to the cycle of tick-borne Lyme disease—at least, in the northeastern and midwestern United States. In a study of mammals on Long Island, New York, researcher Mark Wilson found 93 percent of the adult *Ixodes dammini* ticks on deer and only 7 percent on all the other mammals combined (including dogs and cats). Birds that feed on the ground may play some role in the natural cycle and act as vectors in the spread of *Ixodes* to new territories, but scientists do not yet agree on how great this role may be.

The rapid growth of the suburbs has helped to bring humans into the tick's world. Farms are being replaced by houses, and vast forests are giving way to small wooded areas and lawns with decorative shrubs that deer love to eat. The natural predators that used to keep deer in check have disappeared in the suburbs —either because their homes have been destroyed or because peo-

The suburban environment is contributing to the spread of Lyme disease.

ple considered them too dangerous to have around. Hunting laws protect deer through most of the year. So it should not be surprising that the deer population has exploded from a few hundred thousand at the turn of the century to over fifteen million today. The tick population has exploded along with the deer.

Lyme disease is thus a suburban disease. According to Terry Schulze of the New Jersey State Department of Health, "The majority of cases occur in a backyard setting. There is an 'edge effect', where the wildlife carrying ticks frequent the surrounding bushes, brush and woodpiles."

Can Lyme Disease Spread Without Ticks?

Some scientists believe that Lyme disease may be spread in ways that do not involve *Ixodes* ticks.

For instance, Professor Elizabeth Burgess, who teaches at the School of Veterinary Medicine at the University of Wisconsin, thinks that *B. burgdorferi* can be transmitted by urine and saliva. She and other scientists have found the spirochete in the urine of various animals including horses, dogs, calves, and mice. Even though no ticks were present, infected animals passed on their *Borrelia* bacteria to others boarded with them. Furthermore, Dr. Burgess was able to infect animals with injections of contaminated urine and saliva. Even when infected saliva was placed in the mouths of "healthy" animals, their blood soon showed signs of antibodies against the bacteria.

Dr. Burgess presented her theory at the first Scientific Workshop on Lyme Disease, sponsored by the National Institutes of Health in December, 1988. Dr. Willy Burgdorfer, the discoverer of the Lyme disease bacterium, was at the meeting and mentioned that he himself had developed a Lyme disease rash after being accidentally splashed in the eye by urine from an infected rabbit. The ecology of Lyme disease, he remarked, "is becoming an extremely, extremely complicated story."

Most scientists are waiting for stronger evidence before they will consider urine important in the spread of *Borrelia burgdorferi*. After all, one researcher argued at the meeting, veterinarians and farmers frequently get soaked by animal urine, yet they do not come down with Lyme disease any more often than the general population. Also, others argued, if urine were an important means of transmission, why would the number of cases of Lyme disease reported be the highest just when the *Ixodes* nymphs were biting the most, and not during the winter months when pets and farm animals are usually in close contact with their owners?

Some odd cases have been reported. For instance, one patient insisted he got Lyme disease following a horse bite. But the doctor found no spirochete in the saliva of the horse.

A number of insects, including mosquitoes, deer flies, and horse flies, have been shown to carry the Lyme disease bacterium. Some scientists fear that bites of these insects might provide another means of spreading the disease. But so far there has been no firm evidence that these insects can actually transmit the spirochete to humans. One reason may be that insects such as flies and mosquitoes tend to bite and leave quickly. A tick, on the other hand, remains attached for days, providing more opportunity for infection.

Another troubling possibility is that Lyme disease might be transmitted from infected people to others in blood transfusions. That is what has happened with a far more deadly blood-borne disease, AIDS. So far, there has been no evidence that *Borrelia burgdorferi* has been transmitted to people through transfusions of infected blood. Most experts consider this kind of transmission rather unlikely, but the numbers of cases are still so small that we really can't be sure yet.

If Lyme disease can be transmitted from one person to another by infected blood, then some of the precautions recommended to prevent transmitting AIDS (as well as other blood-borne diseases) would need to be taken. Sharing a toothbrush or a razor might possibly transmit the spirochete if blood from a person carrying it gets into an open cut or sore of someone else. Getting an injection from a doctor should not be a problem, at least in the United States, since single-use, throwaway needles and syringes are routinely used here. Giving blood should not present a danger, either. But getting your ears pierced might be a hazard if the needle is not properly sterilized between operations.

It seems more certain, though, that Lyme disease is *not* transmitted in the other major way that people catch AIDS: through sexual activity. Researchers have not observed any indications that husbands or wives of Lyme disease patients get the disease too (unless they also are bitten by ticks). And while the majority of AIDS cases are concentrated among sexually active young adults, Lyme disease does not show that kind of pattern. Instead, both children and adults can come down with this illness.

We still have much to learn about the roles played by *Ixodes* ticks, the spirochete they carry, and the many vectors that are involved in Lyme disease. But scientists all over the world are studying the problem, and each day we learn a little more.

5.
THE BIOLOGY
OF LYME DISEASE

The deer tick and some of its relatives seem to be the key to the spread of Lyme disease, but ticks are not the real villains in the epidemics that strike each spring and summer. The ticks are merely the carriers of a parasite of their own, the spirochete *Borrelia burgdorferi*. This bacterium is the real cause of the disease, and—researchers are now finding—it does its damage with a lot of help from the victim's own body!

The process starts with a tick bite. It's not a quick hit-and-run attack like the bite of a mosquito or fly, but a slow bloodsucking that may go on for days. The amount of blood taken is huge, compared to the tick, but minor for the victim. Although its elastic abdomen balloons up as it fills with blood,

The female tick on the right is engorged with blood after feeding.

there are limits to how much it can swell. Fortunately (for the tick) it doesn't need all that volume: most of the blood is water, which has no food value for the tick. So as it sucks and swells, its salivary glands pump most of the water back into its host's bloodstream. If the tick is carrying *Borrelia burgdorferi* spirochetes, some of the bacteria go along for the ride. Soon after entering the victim, these spirochetes are spread by the rapidly flowing blood to all parts of the body.

The Body's Defenses

The skin is the human body's first line of defense against bacteria and other microbes that swarm in the world around us. Uncountable numbers of these microscopic creatures are found in the air we breathe, the food we eat, and everything we touch. There are even microbes living on the surface of the body itself. Normally the skin does a pretty good job of keeping unwanted microbes on the outside, but it is no match for the tick's drill-like mouthparts.

Once bacteria have penetrated into the bloodstream—by way of a cut, a burn, or a tick bite—some new lines of body defenders are called up.

First, the injury itself damages body tissues, and they send out chemicals that act as a sort of distress signal. As these chemicals travel through the blood, they trigger a series of reactions. Some of them may raise the body temperature, leading to fever. Others make the walls of tiny blood vessels leaky, so that fluid oozes out of them and makes the tissues swell. These are the reactions of inflammation. They can be very painful and annoying, but they help to make conditions less favorable for the invading microbes to live and multiply. The extra fluid in the swollen tissues also makes it easier for white blood cells, the body's roving disease fighters, to move around.

A variety of white blood cells work together to fight disease germs. These cells are like tiny animated blobs of jelly that can change their shape, bulging out in one direction or drawing inward in another. They can move among the other body cells, swimming in the blood or lymph, creeping through the spaces in tissues, and even squeezing in and out of blood vessels through tiny gaps between cells.

When microbes attack, the first white cell fighters on the scene are several kinds of phagocytes. Their name literally means "eater-cell," and they capture and eat invading bacteria.

Several kinds of lymphocytes are also key fighters in the body's white-cell armies. Some recognize foreign chemicals. (A bacterium, like any other living creature, is made up of many complicated chemicals, a number of which are found in no other kind of organism. They do not match the assortment of chemicals normally present in a healthy human body, and thus they can be recognized as "foreign.") Some lymphocytes attack invading microbes directly and kill them. Others produce special proteins, called antibodies, which can attack microbes. An antibody is a very complicated chemical. It is constructed so that part of it matches perfectly with a part of the foreign chemical (called an antigen). Thus, the two fit together like a key in a lock. The lymphocytes that make antibodies are called B cells. Some of the other lymphocytes (the helper T cells) prompt the B cells to make antibodies; others (suppressor T cells) turn off the B cells' antibody production. Meanwhile, all the various kinds of white cells, which together make up the body's immune system, are busily "talking to each other" by means of chemical signals that help them to coordinate their team efforts.

Battling the Spirochete Invader

When a tick bites a person, sucks up blood, and injects *Borrelia burgdorferi* spirochetes into its victim's bloodstream, the body's defenders are called into action. The damaged tissues send out their chemical distress signals, and the area around the bite becomes red and swollen. Roaming phagocytes flock to the invasion site and attack the bacteria. Meanwhile, lymphocytes are examining the spirochetes to see if they belong in the body or are foreign invaders.

Each bacterium is covered with a protective cell wall, which contains proteins and special chemicals called lipopolysaccharides. (That chemical name sounds complicated, but it just means that they are made up of bits of fat—the "lipo" part—and many sugar molecules—the "saccharides"—bonded together into a large, complex molecule.) These lipopolysaccharides (LPS) are not like any of the normal human body chemicals, but they are rather similar to LPS found on many other disease bacteria. For the body they act as a powerful alarm signal, which prompts some of the white cells to release a substance called interleukin-1 (IL-1). This chemical helps to regulate the response of the immune system to wounds and attacking microbes.

Meanwhile, T lymphocytes have recognized proteins on the bacterial surface as foreign chemicals, and they have alerted B cells to start making antibodies against them. But the process of antibody production is a rather slow one, especially in

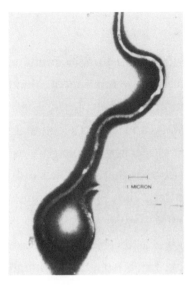

Borrelia burgdorferi,
shown highly magnified
in an electron micrograph.

the case of the *Borrelia* spirochete. It may take four to six weeks after the tick bite that introduced the bacterium in the first place. Furthermore, the spirochete does not stimulate the body's immune system as strongly as many other foreign invaders do.

There are several reasons for this. First of all, the Lyme spirochete is a tricky foe. Researchers believe it may be able to change the chemical makeup of its outer coat. So an antibody made against its first coat may be ineffective against some of the new variations. Studies by Dr. Leonard Sigal, now at Robert Wood Johnson Medical School, UMDNJ, also suggest that *B. burgdorferi* can suppress some of the immune defenses.

In addition, the Lyme disease spirochete can hide in the central nervous system (the spinal cord and brain). Then, months or years later, it may emerge into the bloodstream and cause a whole new outbreak of symptoms.

Turning the Body Against Itself

Researchers believe that many of the worst effects of Lyme disease are due to the mistaken efforts of the body's own de-

47

fense systems. Antibodies against a *Borrelia* protein combine with this bacterial antigen, together with a mixture of blood chemicals called complement, to form immune complexes. These bulky complexes travel through the blood and tend to accumulate in the joints. As they build up, they attract roving phagocytes. These white cells release powerful enzymes that attack not only bacteria but also the bone and cartilage tissues of the joints. The damage they cause results in arthritis-like symptoms.

Dr. Jorge Benach and his colleagues at the New York State Department of Health in Stony Brook, Long Island, have found evidence that interleukin-1 plays a key role in the damaging effects of Lyme disease. The bacterial LPS stimulates the release of IL-1, which prompts the joint tissues to produce a substance called prostaglandin, which causes fever and pain, and also an enzyme, collagenase, which breaks down the connective tissue in the joints.

Meanwhile, some other damaging long-term effects may develop. Because of *Borrelia*'s ability to change its outer coat so frequently, the B lymphocytes keep making new antibodies of different kinds, in the effort to keep up with it. Some of these antibodies may happen to match not only the antigens of the spirochete but also various chemicals of the body's own tissues, such as those in the joints, brain, and muscles. An antibody is not intelligent—it will attack anything that happens to fit into its own "reactive site." If brain cells do, then those brain cells will be injured by the body's own antibodies.

We call such results "autoimmune diseases." They are quite common. One example is rheumatic fever, which can develop as a later result of a simple sore throat. Antibodies produced against the strep throat bacterium happen to match cells in the heart and joints, too. They attack these cells, damaging the heart so that it cannot pump blood as effectively as it used to and causing painful swelling of the joints. These aftereffects of a strep infection, in fact, are quite similar to some of the complications that occur in Lyme disease.

Many of the symptoms of Lyme disease also seem to be just that: the result of the body's antibodies' attack on body tissues. Thus, encephalitis and meningitis, inflammations of brain tissue that may appear in the later stages of Lyme disease, may be the result of antibody action against various parts of the brain. Multiple sclerosis-like symptoms may develop when antibodies are produced against nerve tissue. Studies by Dr. Leonard Sigal and his colleagues at the Lyme Disease Center of Robert Wood Johnson Medical School in New Brunswick, New Jersey, suggest that one compound found in *B. burgdorferi*, flagellin, is very similar to a protein in human nerve tissue. This kind of "molecular mimicry" can result in autoimmune damage as antibodies produced against the bacterial flagellin mistakenly attack nerve tissue, too.

Meanwhile, researchers are working to develop improved tests and treatments for Lyme disease by studying the life habits and body chemistry of the *Ixodes* ticks and the Lyme spirochete and learning more about how they produce their effects on the human body.

6.
SYMPTOMS
OF LYME DISEASE

Christina was a free-lance writer, covering an assignment in Stamford, Connecticut. She was bitten by a tick but didn't think much of it, since aside from the tiny swelling there were no symptoms.

But then, several months later, her world changed. "I couldn't walk four blocks before having to sit down," she recalls. "I was disoriented and I felt very weak. Soon her face became numb and her fingers ached so much, she couldn't use her typewriter. "Some days I'd wake up and my hands would be like claws," she says. "I couldn't pick up a fork." Later Christina developed chest pains and an irregular heartbeat. For six long months her symptoms continued. Finally, except for an occasional numbness, she was able to resume a normal life. But she avoids woody areas, and every time she walks across a grass-covered lawn, she automatically brushes her arms and legs.

Christina is one of thousands who have experienced a nightmare of symptoms after coming down with Lyme disease.

Most people who are bitten don't even realize it. The bite is usually painless, and the nymph that probably was responsible for it is so tiny that it may not be noticed. Hardly larger than the period at the end of this sentence, the nymph may crawl over its victim for many minutes, looking for just the right place to settle down for a meal. Usually its feeding place is on the thighs, under the arms, in the groin area or on the chest.

Stage I

At first a small red rash appears at the point where the tick mouthpart entered through the skin. (By now the tick has gorged itself and dropped off onto the ground.)

For about a third of the victims, nothing more seems to happen. But for the other two-thirds, a variety of symptoms may appear over the next one to four weeks. This is the first of three stages in the development of Lyme disease.

The most unique symptom, and one that is very characteristic of Lyme disease (although not all victims develop it), is a rash that resembles a bull's eye. There is a small red spot where the tick bit, surrounded by a pale circle. Outside this circle is a dark red border. The bull's eye grows larger each day, sometimes reaching as much as a foot or more in diameter. One rash measured more than two feet across! The medical name for this ring-shaped rash is erythema chronicum migrans (ECM) or simply erythema migrans (EM). It means "wandering redness." In many people this name is particularly appropriate, for numerous smaller red spots appear on various parts of the body as

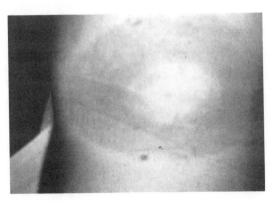

Not all Lyme disease patients develop this typical bull's-eye rash.

the Lyme bacterium multiplies and is carried through the bloodstream.

Days or weeks after the bite, other symptoms may appear. Often these resemble the flu. The person may have a scratchy throat, with a fever. Tiredness may set in, with a vague feeling of illness. Different people may have different combinations of symptoms, including headaches, backaches, nausea, vomiting, chills, swollen lymph glands, loss of appetite, sensitivity to light, a stiff neck, and pain and swelling in the joints, especially the knees.

Then, mysteriously, the symptoms usually disappear, and the person seems to be over the illness. All too often, though, that is not the case. The Lyme victim has merely completed Stage I of the disease. The body's immune system is at work trying to build up a defense against the invading spirochetes. But in doing so, it leads to further damage to the very person it is trying to protect.

Stage II

If the person has not been treated with antibiotics shortly after the encounter with the tick, then in about 10 percent of the cases Stage II sets in. A whole new set of symptoms appears. This may occur weeks or even months after the tick bite. Each Lyme disease victim may experience a different combination of symptoms, depending on which parts of the body are being attacked by its own immune system or by the spirochete.

If the brain or nerves are attacked, which happens in about 10-15 percent of Lyme disease patients, the person may have what seems like a new bout with the same symptoms experienced

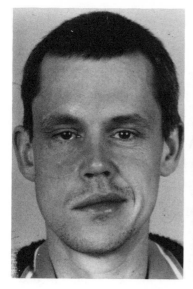 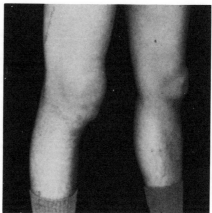

Some symptoms of Lyme disease: Bell's palsy (on the left) and swollen, arthritic knees (on the right).

during Stage I, including headache, nausea, fatigue, and vomiting. The victim may become irritable, getting annoyed at the smallest things. There may be a temporary loss of memory or episodes of forgetfulness and confusion. The person may find all but the dimmest light painful. In very rare serious cases, the victim might become listless and drowsy or even lose consciousness and fall into a coma for a while. Many of these symptoms are those of meningitis and encephalitis, which means that parts of the brain or its covering membranes have become inflamed. Some people experience tingling or numbness in the fingertips or toes. Others suffer from dizziness, weakness in the legs, and sleep problems. They may find they can't concentrate. For some, the muscles in one side (sometimes both sides) of the face seem to droop. They can't smile or show expressions of emotion. Doctors call this condition Bell's palsy.

Some people, during State II, have been misdiagnosed as having multiple sclerosis. In this disease the body's immune system attacks the nerve tissue. The person is unable to control the muscles that are fed by these nerves.

Joint pains are experienced by many victims at this time, especially in the knees. Walking may become very difficult. Many find talking difficult, too, as the jaws swell and ache.

In some unfortunate victims—about 8 percent—the heart is attacked by the spirochete or by the body's own immune system. The inflammation sometimes damages nerves in the heart that act as a pacemaker, setting the rhythm of the heartbeat. The heart may lose its ability to contract properly, resulting in palpitation (fast, thumping beats) or arrythmia (an irregular heartbeat). This can be dangerous. Sometimes an artificial pacemaker has to be inserted, until the inflammation and swelling go down. If this is not done, the patient may continue to experience dizziness, shortness of breath, and might even faint. In most cases the heart complications are not so serious. However, in two of the three reported deaths of Lyme disease victims, heart complications were the cause.

What determines which people suffer from a particular set of symptoms after the bite of a *Borrelia*-infected tick and which ones escape without any serious consequences? Is it just luck?

Researchers have found some evidence that heredity may play an important role. A number of kinds of antigens have been discovered on the surface of human cells. Although each person has a number of specific proteins that are completely unique, found in no one else in the world (except an identical twin), there are also a number of antigens that are typical of particular groups of people.

When researchers studied how various antigens (called the HLA system) are distributed among the different groups, they discovered that some of them seem to be linked with particular diseases. People with tuberculosis, for example, are much more likely to have several specific types of HLA antigens than are members of the general population. This does not mean that the HLA antigens *cause* tuberculosis, merely that they make a person more likely—predisposed—to develop the disease if they are exposed to the bacteria that cause it.

In a similar way, most people with rheumatoid arthritis turn out to be carrying a particular antigen called HLA-DR4. (This antigen is normally found in about a quarter of the population.) When researchers checked Lyme disease victims who had developed severe arthritis, they discovered that these people, too, were likely to have HLA-DR4, as well as another antigen called HLA-DR2. It seems probable that other genetic "markers" will be found to be linked with some of the other Lyme disease symptoms. There may also be genes that provide their carriers with *resistance* to particular diseases, and these may be found in people who recover from Lyme disease without lasting problems.

Stage III

After suffering through Stage II, the Lyme victim often feels relief. Just about all the symptoms may disappear. It seems that the disease has finally been conquered. Instead, the immune system is building up for another assault. Months, even years after that tick bite that started off all the trouble, Stage III may begin.

This is sometimes called the chronic stage, because symptoms can last for years, coming and going without warning.

The joints, the nervous system, and the skin may all become involved at times. But the joints are usually the most troublesome. For somewhat less than 10 percent, chronic arthritis may set in, with the knees attacked most often. Some people find walking very difficult, as their swollen and painful knees refuse to accept the weight of the body on them. The pain and swelling may last for a few days or weeks and then heal. Only the problem returns, time and time again over the years.

If the brain is attacked, the victim may experience temporary memory loss, mood swings, sleep problems, loss of concentration, and various other nervous system problems. In Europe and in the United States, there have been reports of personality disorders and dementia in long-term victims.

Lyme disease patients do not necessarily progress from Stage I to Stage II and then to Stage III. In some cases Stage III may develop without any Stage II symptoms—or even without any previous signs or symptoms of the disease at all!

Perhaps most upsetting of all, for a Lyme disease victim, is that if indeed the disease is conquered through antibiotic treatment, the next tick bite can begin the whole process all over again. When the disease is brought under control at an early stage, the body does not build up an immunity to the Lyme spirochete. Researchers have noticed that some patients develop the typical ECM rash over and over again, as they receive new tick bites. So far, however, no cases have been observed where a rash appeared after Lyme arthritis or neurologic disease had developed. These patients do seem to become immune to further attacks.

7.
DIAGNOSING LYME DISEASE

One day last summer, one of us (A.S.) noticed a bull's-eye rash on his leg. Our family doctor sent a blood sample off for testing but didn't wait for the results. Since we live in a Lyme disease area, and deer roam through our property, he immediately started penicillin treatments. The test came back negative, but "that doesn't mean much," the doctor said. There have been no further symptoms since then, except for a mysterious hot swelling in a finger joint that went away after a week or two. We still don't know whether it was just a false alarm.

Lyme disease, like other diseases, is best treated in its earliest stages, before much damage has been done to the body. But an illness has to be diagnosed before it can be treated. It's easy for a doctor to diagnose a broken arm. A break in the bone shows up clearly on an X-ray. Lyme disease isn't as easy to determine. The symptoms that can result from a *Borrelia* infection are so varied that they could be caused by many different illnesses, ranging from the flu to heart disease or cancer. The bull's-eye rash that could prompt a doctor to suspect Lyme disease may be mistaken for a bug bite, or even a poison ivy rash or ringworm. One study found that only 40 percent of Lyme disease patients had a rash at all. Unless a doctor has seen many cases in the area, he or she might not even think of Lyme disease as a possible cause. For this reason, some people have gone to doctor after doctor, sometimes over several years, before their Lyme disease was correctly diagnosed.

Linda Hanner of Minnesota saw twenty-nine specialists over a six-year period, before it was determined she had Lyme disease. Vickie Womack of Mendocino, California spent $20,000 in medical bills in three years before her Lyme disease was discovered. "It has been frustrating to be termed a hypochondriac, and to be told by doctors what you really need is a psychiatrist," she said.

Beckie and Todd Murdock were almost relieved when they were told their entire family had Lyme disease. After more than a year of persistant flu symptoms, joint aches, and fatigue, the Murdocks and their three children were finally given an explanation for their sufferings. "We could finally say, 'This is what was wrong with us.'" Initial Lyme disease tests had indicated negative results, but the Murdocks persisted. "You have to be patient with the doctor," Todd Murdock said. "With this, they can't give you a blood test and say, 'Yes you're pregnant.'"

Why has Lyme disease been so hard to diagnose? After all, there are blood tests for Lyme disease. Unfortunately, in many cases these blood tests are not completely reliable. In fact, researchers believe the current tests detect only half of all confirmed Lyme disease cases.

Lyme Disease Tests

Many tests for diseases are done by testing a patient's blood or urine. Technicians examine the samples in different ways. Sometimes they look for the microorganisms that can be causing an illness. Measuring the amounts of various kinds of blood cells or particular blood chemicals and comparing the results to a "normal" sample may give diagnostic clues. A common type of diagnostic test checks for antibodies to a disease microbe, to determine whether the body has been exposed to it and has mounted defenses against it. There are many different ways to conduct each kind of test, as well. Some tests are quick and simple, yielding results in a few minutes in the doctor's office. Others require sophisticated and expensive equipment and must be run by highly skilled technicians.

Using a microscope to look for *Borrelia* bacteria would seem the most obvious way to tell if a person's blood is infected with the spirochete. Unfortunately, finding a particular microbe in a blood specimen is not so easy. A test tube full of blood contains so few bacteria, even during an active infection, that it would be very much like looking for a needle in a haystack. One way to increase the chances of finding *Borrelia*— if it is there—is to "culture" the blood sample. The spiro-

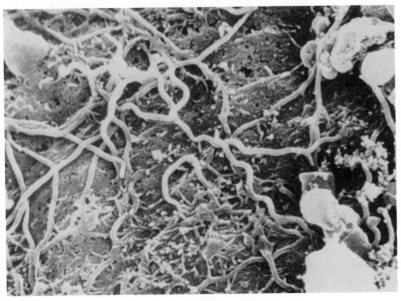

Micrograph of *Borrelia burgdorferi* spirochetes.

chetes are provided with an ideal environment to reproduce, and over a period of weeks they multiply until there are enough of them present to measure. The process takes time before the results are available. Such tests can also be misleading if the original sample didn't happen to contain any of the spirochetes, even though there were some present in the body.

For these reasons, the currently available Lyme disease tests generally look for antibodies that a healthy person's immune system would produce to fight the *Borrelia* bacteria. There are about a dozen different blood tests used in laboratories around the country. Most of them are based on two methods, IFA and ELISA.

In the IFA method (immunofluorescence assays), *B. burgdorferi* bacteria are killed and placed on a microscope slide. A sample of the patient's blood is then added. If the blood contains antibodies, they will attach themselves to the bacterial proteins. A reagent that glows under ultraviolet light is added to make the results easier to detect. (The antibodies show up in a glowing green under an ultraviolet microscope.) The titer or concentration of antibodies present is calculated from the amount of green fluorescence. But the IFA test is not always accurate. Other antibodies that happen to be present in the blood can attach themselves to the bacteria, causing a green glow when the reagent is added. Moreover, the test is rather subjective—the technician determines how much fluorescence is present. Automated versions of IFAs, in which a machine measures the amount of fluorescence, are now being developed and should make the test more objective and accurate.

ELISA (enzyme-linked immunosorbent assay) tests work in a similar way, but the ELISA process is completely automated.

B. burgdorferi proteins are separated and placed into an ELISA plate that contains 96 plastic wells. The patient's blood sample is added to the wells in the plate. Once again, if the blood sample contains *Borrelia* antibodies, they will attach to the proteins in the wells. An enzyme reagent that changes color if antibodies are present provides a result that can be read automatically by a machine. The amount of color indicates the level of antibodies present. However, the laboratory has to establish a "normal" level for a certain area, because no samples, even from noninfected people, will be completely negative.

Both ELISA and IFA tests require sophisticated equipment and highly trained technicians, and the reagents aren't cheap.

How Accurate Are the Results?

The biggest problem with antibody tests is that it takes time for the body to produce antibodies against an invading microbe. In Lyme disease, antibodies may not appear in large enough quantities to be measured for four to six weeks after the tick passes the infection through the skin. Therefore, the blood test is not very useful in detecting Lyme disease in the early stages— the time when a correct diagnosis and treatment would be most effective!

Some people don't develop many antibodies even in the later stages. Dr. Russell Johnson, a microbiologist at the University of Minnesota, explains that in some people the immune response does not react very strongly to Lyme disease bacteria, and antibodies do not build up significantly. This can cause "false negative" results (that is, a negative test result when infection is actually present) at any stage of the disease. In addition, if a person takes antibiotics for another illness while *Borrelia* is present, the dosage may not be enough to kill the Lyme bacteria but enough to hinder the immune response and prevent antibodies from building up to high enough levels to be measured by the Lyme disease test. This would give a "false negative" test result, even though the organism is still active in the body.

Dr. Stephen E. Schutzer at the University of Medicine and Dentistry of New Jersey recently discovered another reason for false negative test results. In most diseases, some free antibodies typically circulate in the blood, and these are picked up in the antibody tests. But in Lyme disease, often all of the antibodies are bound up with *B. burgdorferi* antigens in immune complexes, which the standard tests do not detect. Blood samples from such patients do test positive when they are treated with special procedures to split the immune complexes apart. The researchers suggest that such a retesting procedure might become a routine check in cases when doctors strongly suspect Lyme disease but the standard blood test is negative.

In routine antibody tests, "false positives" (positive test results when the person is not actively infected with *B. burgdorferi)* are also possible. The tests are not completely specific for the Lyme disease microbe and may also react to antigens of other bacteria. Moreover, people who have had Lyme disease still have high antibody levels for awhile and may give false positive results for months or years after being cured.

According to Dr. Louis Magnarelli, a medical entomologist at the Connecticut Agricultural Experiment Station, many of the current tests are only 10-15 percent accurate before three weeks, 30 percent accurate for patients in Stage I at more than three weeks after infection, 50-60 percent accurate in Stage 2 patients with Bell's palsy, encephalitis, or meningitis, and 85-90 percent accurate in late stages when arthritis is present.

To further complicate the problem, patients may test negative according to the results of one lab and positive at another. A study of outdoor workers in New Jersey, for example, conducted by researchers at the New Jersey Department of Health, the University of Pennsylvania, and the Harvard School of Public Health, compared results of samples sent to four different laboratories. A blood sample from each person was examined by each lab. The researchers found that the test results varied greatly from one lab to another, and even in the same lab. When the Minnesota State Health Department tested seventeen forestry workers after a fellow worker contracted Lyme disease, they also sent samples to four separate labs. The results ranged from zero positives at one lab to six positives at another.

There are many laboratories that perform blood analyses, and some experts believe that many of them should not be conducting Lyme disease tests. "Unless a doctor can verify that the laboratory is proficient at doing the Lyme disease test, it is a waste of money to do it," says Dr. Michael T. Osterholm, chief epidemiologist for the Minnesota State Health department. A major problem is that there are no national standards, and each lab sets up its own quality controls to determine how much antibody in a sample indicates an infection is present. Some of the tests also require a subjective evaluation by the technician, and this can vary from technician to technician, and even from day to day with the same technician.

No one is quite sure how many Lyme disease tests are performed each year throughout the country, but about 90,000 tests

63

were run in New Jersey in 1988 at a cost of $3.5 million. Many experts are quite concerned about the lack of standardization and the confusion it is adding to the Lyme disease dilemma. In response to the problem, the CDC and state health officials formed a committee late in 1989 to discuss what steps need to be taken to help standardize and improve the quality of Lyme disease testing.

Because of the limitations of the Lyme disease tests, experts advise doctors to combine the tests with clinical observations when making their diagnosis. Dr. Patrick Moore of the Centers for Disease Control says the diagnosis should be based on the patient's symptoms and case history as well. Some doctors will prescribe antibiotics right away, if they have a strong suspicion of Lyme disease—before they get blood test results, and even if the results come back negative. Many experts agree, and they advise this procedure when the symptoms seem to fit the description of Lyme disease.

The Great Masquerader

But just what symptoms "seem to fit" Lyme disease? We have already seen that the classic telltale sign—a bull's-eye rash —doesn't always occur. In some cases a rash will disappear, and the disease can resurface months or years later with severe complications like heart problems, neurological disorders, and arthritis. And all of the symptoms that Lyme disease patients experience are the same symptoms that can occur in numerous other diseases. In fact, there are more than a dozen ailments that have been wrongly diagnosed when Lyme disease was really at fault. Lyme disease has been called the Great Imitator and

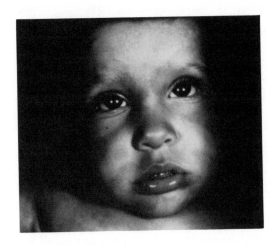

Lyme disease
often strikes
children.

Great Masquerader for good reason!

Lyme disease has been mistaken for Bell's palsy, meningitis, gout, chronic fatigue, multiple sclerosis, rheumatic fever, and viral infections like the flu. One of the most common misdiagnoses is juvenile rheumatoid arthritis (JRA). A report from the University Hospital of the State University of New York at Stony Brook found that in areas where Lyme disease is firmly established, up to 25 percent of children who were diagnosed with JRA really have Lyme disease instead.

This is quite serious, because in most cases Lyme disease is curable, even in late stages, but the tissue damage it causes can be irreversible. There is no cure for JRA. So patients who were incorrectly given that diagnosis when they really have Lyme disease are being deprived of effective treatments that could spare them unnecessary pain and disability. Some health officials are suggesting that all parents of children who were diagnosed with JRA should immediately have their child tested for Lyme disease just to make sure. This is especially urgent for those who live in or have visited Lyme disease "hot spots," and those whose children were diagnosed with JRA before the late 1980s when doctors and the public became more aware of Lyme disease.

Researchers at several laboratories have been examining the spinal fluid of patients with various kinds of nervous system disorders. In some cases they have found antibodies to the Lyme spirochete, even when antibodies were not present in the blood. Not only are the spinal taps more accurate than blood tests in such cases, the researchers say, but doctors can also use them to determine whether the antibodies got into the spinal fluid from the blood or are actually being produced in the nervous system. The distinction is important, says Dr. Michael E. Finkel of the Western Wisconsin Lyme Disease Center in Eau Claire, Wisconsin, because people with an active infection of the nervous system need to receive antibiotics by intravenous injections rather than pills taken by mouth.

Before concluding that a patient has Lyme disease, a doctor has to rule out numerous other ailments. The fact that the tests for Lyme disease are unreliable makes this all the more difficult. Thus, it is no surprise that many health officials are claiming that Lyme disease is being severely underdiagnosed. But there are experts who believe that because of the hysteria that has built up over the last few years, doctors are *over*diagnosing the disease. They feel that some people are being treated for Lyme disease who don't really have it. Dr. Raymond Dattwyler of the Lyme Disease Center at SUNY Stony Brook claims, "What we're seeing is a pop disease." This can be dangerous, because a person may have a more serious condition that needs a different kind of treatment; but the real problem may not be diagnosed because the patient and doctor are convinced that Lyme disease is the problem.

How Much Testing?

Just how long should a person persist in trying to determine whether he or she has Lyme disease when blood tests come back negative? Experts' opinions differ. But if symptoms persist and other causes cannot be found, some experts suggest you insist on periodic tests for the disease, or suggest to your doctor that the blood sample be sent to a second lab that uses a different type of test, or to a specialized Lyme disease research lab.

No one knows for sure exactly how many people have been misdiagnosed with other "incurable" illnesses and are needlessly suffering, since Lyme disease *is* curable. But the numbers are alarming enough for some experts, like Dr. Andrew Pachner, a neurologist and Lyme disease specialist at Georgetown University, to suggest that Lyme disease tests should become more routinely used. "Anybody in an area endemic for Lyme disease who develops neurological problems should be tested." Many hospitals routinely check patients who are admitted for syphilis. Dr. Pachner believes that all hospital patients in "hot spot" areas should also be tested for Lyme disease.

Lyme disease tests are becoming more and more sophisticated. As they improve, some of the confusion surrounding the disease should clear up, as well.

Improved Lyme Disease Tests

Two new Lyme disease tests were approved by the Food and

Drug Administration (FDA) in late 1989. Some health officials believe these new antibody tests may be more accurate than previously available tests. One of them can be performed right in the doctor's office, with results in six or seven minutes. (Most Lyme disease blood tests must be sent out to a lab and take a week before the doctor gets the results.)

Meanwhile, experts are hopeful that new, more effective tests are on the way. Research is being conducted on ways to detect Lyme disease at early stages.

Some researchers are looking into methods of detecting the disease without looking for antibodies. One of these involves looking for the actual spirochete in blood or urine samples by looking for the bacterial antigens. Antigens can be detected even before antibodies are formed. This type of test is the opposite of the IFA and ELISA procedures. Test samples are mixed with prepared *antibodies*, and a reaction indicates that the antigens are present. Dr. Russell Johnson and colleagues at the University of Minnesota have been working with the 3M Company to develop an antigen urine test. Dr. Russell's preliminary tests were able to detect the antigens in urine in both early and late stages of Lyme disease.

Dr. Raymond Dattwyler and his colleagues at the Lyme Disease Center at SUNY Stony Brook have developed a blood test based on measurements of the response of the body's immune system T cells. This test can detect Lyme disease when antibody response has not been strong, or when the patient has taken antibiotics, and antibodies are not present. If the body's T lymphocytes recognize *Borrelia* bacteria, they will divide and grow, and this response can be measured very accurately. Comparisons of T-cell reactivity in the joint fluid or spinal fluid to that in the blood can also spotlight possible local infections, as demonstrated in studies by Dr. Leonard Sigal of Robert Wood Johnson Medical School, UMDNJ. However, the test has to be conducted within twenty-four hours after the blood is taken, and it requires very sophisticated instrumentation and expertise. The test has another drawback: anyone who has ever been exposed to the bacteria—even years ago—will test positive.

Researchers at the Rocky Mountain Laboratories in Montana, Patricia A. Rosa and Tom G. Schwan have found an extremely reliable way to look for Lyme disease bacteria. Using a technique called PCR (polymerase chain reaction) they were able to detect the bacteria in samples that contained as little as five microscopic spirochetes. The technique involves identifying trace amounts of DNA (the substance of the genes) from the microbes. The researchers were able to detect seventeen out of eighteen *Borrelia burgdorferi* strains that came from around the world, and a slight modification also permitted the detection of the eighteenth. This is quite a significant advance, because some people with a slightly different strain of the microorganism give a negative result with current tests.

The PCR technique is patented by the Cetus Corporation of Emeryville, California. In the procedure, primers—two tiny pieces of genetic material—are used as markers on the ends of a segment of *B. burgdorferi* DNA. If the *B. burgdorferi* DNA is present in a test sample, an enzyme called a polymerase causes a chain reaction that repeatedly copies the DNA strand until there is enough to be easily identified.

Since the announcement by the Montana researchers late in 1989, other researchers have been racing to use the technique to develop a commercial PCR test. One of the questions that need to be answered is just where the test sample should be taken from. Human tissue samples contain few, if any, spirochetes, and the place with the largest number of microorganisms needs to be determined.

The Rocky Mountain researchers hope to use PCR to uncover some other mysteries of Lyme disease. For example, some patients never get severe symptoms, but others develop heart problems and neurological complications. Why? Does the bacterium change to a form the immune system cannot recognize, thus causing more problems even after the body's defenses build up antibodies? Or are the complications an autoimmune response that is triggered after the infection is defeated?

Diagnosing an Epidemic

For now, doctors will diagnose the disease to the best of their ability, while researchers continue to work on approaches that will aid in diagnosing the disease. But when it comes to reporting diagnosed cases to the government so that health officials can see how serious the problem is, the situation becomes even more confusing.

Although most states require reporting of Lyme disease cases, not all do. And many doctors might not bother because there is a lot of paperwork involved. Another reason researchers believe the reported number of cases is much lower than the actual number is that the CDC guidelines for diagnosing Lyme disease are very strict. These strict requirements were set to keep the statistics uniform and consistent, but many researchers believe they cause the reported totals to greatly underestimate the actual number of cases that are occurring.

There are two sets of criteria to use in determining whether a case meets the CDC standards for confirmation of Lyme disease.

In endemic areas (that is, where Lyme disease is known to be occurring):

1) the bull's-eye rash must be present, and the person must have been exposed to an endemic region within the past 30 days.

2) if there is no bull's-eye rash, a blood test must be positive and at least one organ system must be involved (neurological complications, heart problems, arthritis, etc.)

In nonendemic areas (that is, where Lyme disease is not common):

1) there must be a bull's-eye rash *and*:

2,A) a blood test must test positive *or*

2,B) two organ systems must be affected.

(As this book was going to press, a new case definition for Lyme disease was being considered. The new criteria should resolve many of the current problems.)

8.
TREATMENT
OF LYME DISEASE

Lyme disease can sometimes clear up on its own, after a period of several months. That is the opinion of a number of health experts, including Stony Brook immunologist Dr. Raymond Dattwyler. Some people might not even know they were infected before the disease is gone from their bodies. In Europe this bacterial infection has been around for a century, and treatments have not always been available. Dr. Klaus Hansen, a Danish immunologist, says that in Denmark "there was no treatment, but people recovered anyway." He points out that even though many cases were untreated, long-lasting complications are quite rare in Denmark. However, Dr. Dattwyler notes that in about one in twenty untreated cases, complications like severe chronic arthritis can develop.

Antibiotics

European doctors first treated the disease with antibiotics. Today doctors in America also use antibiotic treatments to fight the disease. But there is still much debate about which treatments work the best, and doctors have their own preferences.

Typically, antibiotics are taken either by mouth (orally) or by injection. Swallowing a pill or liquid by mouth is certainly easier and more convenient. The patient can pick up a supply at a local pharmacy and take the medication at home or

72

even at school or work. But anything that is swallowed goes down into the stomach, where powerful chemicals in an acid bath start to work on it. A few substances are absorbed directly from the stomach into the bloodstream, but most continue their travels through the digestive system, passing into the small intestines. There a different assortment of chemicals works to break them down. So an oral drug may be changed before it ever gets into the bloodstream, or only a portion of it may be absorbed into the blood. Injecting an antibiotic delivers it faster and bypasses the digestive reactions. It may be injected into a muscle, from which it passes into the tiny blood vessels that supply the muscle cells. Or the doctor may inject it directly into a vein (intravenously), delivering it immediately to the place where it will do its job. Injections can thus be much more effective, but generally they are not a do-it-yourself project.

Oral antibiotics shorten the amount of time a Lyme disease patient will have a rash and other early symptoms. They can also prevent advanced symptoms in most patients when given during the early stages of the disease. In fact, according to some experts, when antibiotics are given within the first week to ten days after a tick bite, further complications are avoided in nearly every case. Other experts disagree, reporting that up to half of their patients continue to experience headaches, fatigue, and achy joints and muscles for months or years after the initial infection. When treatment is delayed because the disease is not diagnosed, serious complications can develop, and permanent damage to the body is possible.

According to Dr. Dattwyler, patients who develop the bull's-eye rash but have no other symptoms generally are completely cured when treated early with antibiotics. People who develop infections in the central nervous system, resulting in a stiff neck or severe headaches, also have a cure rate approaching 100 percent when treated early, although it often takes up to three months before the patient recovers fully.

In general, antibiotics have been successful in all stages of Lyme disease, but treatment is quickest and most effective during the early stage. Patients suffering from later stages of the disease may have to receive intravenous antibiotics for two weeks. More than 50 percent of those with arthritis who are not treated until the later stages may not respond to treatment, and their symptoms may continue for some time.

Experts stress the need to cure the disease as quickly as possible, to have the best chance of a complete cure and to prevent tissue damage. But some doctors are more willing than

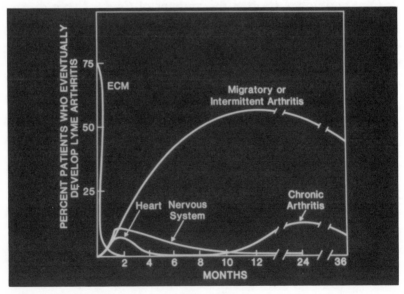

Symptoms of Lyme disease develop at different rates.

others to prescribe antibiotics. Some will do so only when the patient shows definite symptoms. Dr. Joseph Burnett, head of dermatology at the University of Maryland School of Medicine in Baltimore, suggests that all patients with bites from ticks suspected of causing Lyme disease should be treated within thirty days of being bitten. Some doctors even give antibiotics as a preventive measure when a patient will be visiting a Lyme disease hot spot area, although most specialists do not feel this is advisable.

Some Drug Therapies for Lyme Disease

Oral tetracycline or doxycycline is often prescribed for adults (except for pregnant women) and for children over eight years old. The drug is given for a period of ten days to three weeks, but some people don't respond. Amoxicillin is usually prescribed for younger children, and for pregnant or breast-feeding mothers. Penicillin V is also used. Erythromycin is usually prescribed for patients allergic to tetracyclines and penicillins, but it is often less effective.

Some doctors believe that tetracycline, penicillin, and erythromycin are not good choices for early treatments. They recommend doxycycline, or a combination of amoxicillin plus probenecid for use during early stages of Lyme disease. (Probenecid keeps penicillin and amoxicillin circulating in the blood at high concentrations.)

At Stony Brook, Dr. Raymond Dattwyler and his colleagues found that some patients treated with low doses of antibiotics can develop a chronic infection that makes them feel constantly tired and ill and produces negative results on Lyme disease blood tests. The reason is that if the antibiotic treatment is not strong enough, not all the microorganisms will be killed, but meanwhile the antibiotic prevents the body from building up a detectable level of antibodies. Low-dose antibiotics used to be the recommended treatment, but the Stony Brook researchers abandoned this practice in the mid-1980s and now administer higher doses for early-stage patients. They warn, however, that some doctors may still be using the older treatment.

For those who have progressed to Stage II Lyme disease, oral tetracycline, doxycycline, or amoxicillin may be used for a month to treat mild cases. In more severe cases involving meningitis, encephalitis, or heart problems, some specialists recommend two weeks of intravenous penicillin.

Some doctors believe ceftriaxone and cefotaxime may be more effective. These are antibiotics from the cephalosporin family. They are used particularly when there are neurological complications. These drugs penetrate into the central nervous system to help fight the spirochetes that have settled in there. The treatment costs more than $1000 a week for a two-week regimen. Costs are relative, though. These cephalosporin antibiotics may be given on an outpatient basis, whereas other treatments require a long hospital stay—which can cost far more.

In some cases, following hospitalization, patients administer the drugs intravenously to themselves at home. They inject them through a tube called a catheter inserted under the skin; this tube has to be changed by a nurse every few days to prevent infections.

Pregnant women are a special case, for a Lyme disease infection might harm not only the woman herself but her unborn child, as well. A pregnant woman who suspects she might have Lyme disease should get treatment as soon as possible. Treatment in such cases usually includes a high dosage of oral amoxicillin or intravenous penicillin or ceftriaxone.

In Stage III patients, two to three weeks of intravenous penicillin is sometimes effective, but the results might not be visible for several months. Ceftriaxone may be given intravenously to those who don't respond to penicillin. Amoxicillin with probenecid is also being used for severe arthritis.

One reason there is so much confusion and disagreement about which treatment plans work best is that Lyme disease symptoms vary so much from one person to another. Some of the symptoms patients complain of may not even be due to Lyme disease. Laboratory studies aren't always very useful, either. For example, erythromycin kills *Borrelia* bacteria most effectively in the test tube. But clinical tests with humans suggest that tetracycline and penicillin may be more effective. As new drug companies enter the battle against Lyme disease, researchers feel hopeful that better treatment plans are not far off.

Treating the Late Complications

In addition to antibiotic treatments, more specialized drugs and therapies may be needed in the later stages, when the disease is attacking various parts of the body. Treatments are targeted to specific complications of advanced Lyme disease. Antiinflammatory drugs such as steroids and aspirin, for example, help reduce swelling and inflammation. Cortisone injections, draining of fluid, and even surgery may be employed to reduce swollen joints. Exercise, hot and cold packs, and other physical rehabilitation treatments can help to rebuild deteriorated muscles and body tissue. Antidepressant drugs are used for patients suffering from severe clinical depression. Antipsychotic drugs are prescribed for the rare patients with hallucinations and other symptoms of mental disorders.

What to Expect after Treatment Begins

Following treatment, a patient's response can be very unpredictable. Some find their symptoms clear up right away. Others have lingering problems. Sometimes relapses occur, requiring additional treatment, and sometimes they clear up on their own.

Some patients have an especially discouraging experience: After the treatments begin, the symptoms suddenly seem to get much worse! Roughly one out of six patients may experience fever, chills, muscle pains, low blood pressure, or sore throat, twenty-four hours after taking penicillin or tetracycline. (This result doesn't happen as often with erythromycin.) Doctors call this the Jarisch-Herxheimer reaction. A similar reaction also occurs in the treatment of other spirochete-caused diseases, such as syphilis.

Dr. David Volkman of Stony Brook explains the Jarisch-Herxheimer reaction as the body's response in the battle agains the microorganisms. Large numbers of spirochetes are killed, all at once. As their dead bodies break down, poisons are released and act on the body tissues. Large amounts of bacterial lipopolysaccharides (LPS), for example, stimulate the production of body chemicals that promote fever and pain. Usually the response occurs within twenty-four hours after the beginning of therapy and goes away within another twenty-four hours. The response may be frustrating for the patient, but doctors generally consider it a sign that the antibiotic is working.

Drug Side-Effects

Tetracycline and other antibiotics are generally safe, but there can be side-effects. The antibiotics kill the *Borrelia* bacteria in the body, but they also kill "good bacteria"—in the large intestine, for example. Patients taking tetracycline may have diarrhea, and women may develop vaginal yeast infections. (When the bacteria that normally live in the body are killed off, yeasts and other microbes that are not sensitive to the antibiotic may multiply wildly.) People who are allergic to the drug may have serious allergic reactions. Tetracycline can make people extremely sensitive to sunlight, a side effect that poses special problems in the summer. Any troublesome symptoms should be reported immediately to a doctor, who may prescribe a different antibiotic.

When Treatments Fail

More and more often, doctors are seeing cases in which the standard treatments for Lyme disease do not seem to be effective. Symptoms persist even after repeated regimens of intravenous antibiotics.

Claire Palermo, for example, spent $30,000 for medical treatments but continued to suffer from numerous symptoms including arthritis, heart palpitations, fatigue, and depression.

Another sufferer, Frank Zeoli, was given antibiotics when he developed a rash even though his blood test was negative. Six months later the thirty-two-year-old had to leave his job as a tree cutter because of nausea and disorientation. He had his blood tested again, and this time it was positive for Lyme disease. The doctors put him on an intravenous treatment for two weeks. But headaches, joint aches, nausea, and fatigue continued, even after another doctor prescribed oral antibiotics. Finally, "The doctor told me I should just try living with it until a new treatment came out."

Experts claim that when Lyme disease is detected early, most cases are cured with antibiotics. But 10-25 percent of late-diagnosed cases do not respond to strong doses of intravenous antibiotics. (Some specialists report a success rate of only 50 percent.) "To be honest, I don't know what to do with patients who have recurrent symptoms after they've been treated, and I don't think anyone else does either," says Dr. Thomas Rush, director of the Phelps Late Lyme Center in North Tarrytown, New York.

Dr. Allen Steere, who first described Lyme disease in America, has treated more than 1500 people. He has found that most of the patients who were treated soon after symptoms began recovered very quickly after treatment. More progressed cases, involving the nervous system and body joints, typically recover more slowly. Why don't antibiotics help in some cases? Dr. Steere suggests that some people's heredity makes them susceptible to an autoimmune response that causes the body to work against itself. Such autoimmune reactions can produce arthritis, which continues after the infection has been removed from the body. Another theory, Dr. Steere points out, is "that the organism is able to hide out in such a way that antibiotics can't reach it." One hiding place might be the nervous system. In a number of other diseases, including herpes, chickenpox (which later may recur as shingles), and syphilis, an invading microorganism settles down in nerve tissue after the first acute infection is over. Years later it may emerge to produce a new round of symptoms.

Although some Lyme disease sufferers are not helped by the treatments available today, new drugs are being explored for patients who don't respond to normal therapies. Researchers are hopeful that eventually all cases will be treatable.

Can People Develop Immunity to Lyme Disease?

Researchers are still not sure whether a person can ever develop an immunity to Lyme disease. In most infectious diseases, after a person has been exposed to a microorganism and builds up antibodies to it, the person becomes "immune" to that disease. Some of the antibodies are kept on file in special "memory cells," and if the same kind of microbe invades the body again, the person can quickly fight it off. This is the basis of modern vaccinations: A small dose of antigens, perhaps specially modified so they cannot cause illness, is injected so that the person can build up an immunity to a disease without having to suffer through an active case of it. But people seem to be able to be reinfected with Lyme disease even after it has been cured.

Is this "reinfection" just a relapse of the original infection? Or did the person ever build up antibodies in the first place? Perhaps the antibody immunity formed after the first infection was only temporary. Opinions vary among the experts. Some point out that syphilis patients do not build up immunity to the disease when treated at an early stage. Because this spirochete infection is similar to Lyme disease in other ways, some researchers believe it may also be impossible to develop immunity to Lyme disease.

If that is true, efforts to develop a protective vaccine against Lyme disease may be doomed to failure. But experimental vaccines are being developed, and animal experiments have shown some promise. Dr. Russell Johnson at the University of Minnesota was able to successfully vaccinate hamsters against *Borrelia* infection. Injections of killed spirochetes before exposure to live bacteria helped to block infection, but antibodies given to already infected hamsters were ineffective.

Researchers will have to find ways of getting around the spirochete's ability to change its outer coat before really effective Lyme disease vaccines can be produced; most experts believe that such an achievement is not likely in the very near future.

9.
PROTECTING AGAINST LYME DISEASE

The only way to make sure you won't be bitten by a tick that carries Lyme disease is to avoid going anywhere these ticks might be. But the ticks and the disease are spreading, and it is becoming increasingly difficult to avoid them. Ticks lurk in tall grass, in brush and bushes, and in the woods, but they can also be found on well kept lawns. Many people are bitten in their own backyards. Even if you decided to hide in your bed, you might still be bitten by a tick that hitched a ride inside on someone else's clothes, or in the fur of a pet cat or dog.

Sensible Precautions

The most sensible thing to do is to be prepared. Take precautions when you visit places where ticks are known to be plentiful. When you walk in tall grass or woods, walk the dog, or work on garden shrubs and bushes, wear clothes that will help prevent ticks from reaching your skin. Ticks crawl upward from the ground or from blades of grass or shrubs. So it is important to keep the lower part of your body covered. It's best not to go barefoot; instead, wear closed shoes, sneakers, or boots. It might be a temptation to go out in shorts or a swimsuit on a hot summer day, but if you are in tick country you could be asking for trouble. It is safer to wear long pants and long-sleeved shirts, with the shirt bottom tucked into the pants. Tucking the bottoms of your pants legs into your socks provides further tick-proofing. Tight cuffs and collars are best, so that the ticks can't crawl inside. Some experts suggest a rubber band around pant and shirt cuffs to make it even harder for ticks—but make sure it doesn't cut off your circulation. Wear light-colored clothing because the tiny tick is easier to see against a light background.

When hiking, don't go off the trail. Stay to the center, away from shrubs and other vegetation where ticks might be lurking. Check your clothes often and brush off any specks you see. Remember the adult tick is about the size of a sesame seed, and in the nymph stage that is most likely to transmit the Lyme spirochete to humans it is only as large as a poppy seed. One health official recommends: "look for a freckle that moves."

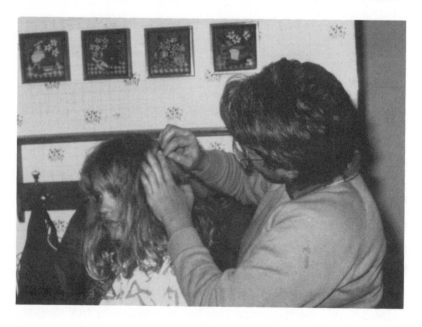

Check carefully for ticks after coming in from outdoors.

When you get home, wash your clothes and take a shower to wash off any unattached ticks. Then inspect your body, including your scalp, hair, neck, in and behind your ears, underarms, groin area, behind your knees, and your lower legs and arms. Check your back and the back of your head with a mirror, or have someone look for you.

Many people live in areas that are known to have large populations of *Ixodes* ticks. People in these endemic areas have different reactions to the Lyme disease problem. Some decide to move away to a different part of the country. But as the disease spreads, it is not likely that any place will stay totally safe from Lyme disease. Besides, other areas that currently have few cases of Lyme disease have other health problems of their own. People are worried about radon, contaminated water, carcinogens in the air, crime and drugs, tornadoes and hurricanes—the list of concerns is almost endless.

Some people in endemic regions just shrug and say there's nothing they can do about it. They go on living the way they always have. Some decide to take daily precautions to avoid being bitten by ticks, and do everything they can to eliminate or reduce the tick population in their surroundings.

Health experts advise that those living in Lyme disease hot spots should take precautions every day, especially during the summer season when the ticks are most active and people spend the most time outdoors. Family members should be checked frequently for ticks, especially before going to sleep at night. Some doctors suggest that people who live in Lyme disease hot spots should be sure to shower every day. Deer ticks tend to crawl around on the skin for awhile before attaching themselves. Even after a tick is attached, it may not transmit the bacteria

The tall grass by the side of the road may be harboring ticks.

right away. Showering can wash off unattached ticks and help you to notice attached ones before they can do any harm.

If pets go outside, they may bring ticks into the house. Cats and dogs should be brushed every day, preferably outside. They should wear tick collars to help keep ticks off. Ask your veterinarian for a safe repellent for spraying on your pet when you go for a walk. You should never walk your pet in tall grass, in the woods or in thick brush. Health experts recommend that pets should not be allowed on furniture, and they shouldn't sleep in bed with you—just in case some unwelcome guests are hiding in their fur.

Tick Repellents

Insect repellents applied to the skin or clothing can provide some additional protection against ticks for people who go hiking or camping. The repellents that contain DEET (diethyltoluamide, which may also appear on labels as diethyl-M-toluamide or N,N-diethy-meta-toluamide) are recommended as the best and safest. However, *The Medical Letter*, a professional publication about drugs, cautions that in large amounts, DEET repellents can cause allergic or toxic reactions. (Up to 15 percent of the chemical can be absorbed into the skin and there have been reports of seizures, especially in children.) Experts advise that only repellents with DEET concentrations of 50 percent or less should be applied to the skin. In fact, some experts advise against putting *any* repellents directly on the skin, particularly for children.

Solutions containing up to 100 percent DEET can safely be applied to clothing, especially on shoes, socks, and at tick "entry points" like pant and shirtsleeve cuffs, where ticks can crawl inside. Because some people are sensitive to DEET repellents, a small amount should always be tested first to see if there is any reaction. The repellents should also be tested on clothing because they can damage certain synthetic fabrics.

Over-the-counter products that contain DEET include Ben's 100, Cutter, Muskol, Off! and Deep Woods Off!, 6/12, and Tick Garde.

Another product, called Permanone Tick Repellent, actually kills ticks. The active ingredient of Permanone is permethrin, a synthetic variation of natural insecticides, pyrethrins, found in African chrysanthemums. The natural pyrethrins break down easily in sunlight, but the synthetic permethrin resists sunlight and lasts up to four weeks. Unlike DEET which washes off when you sweat or go swimming, permethrin is water resistant, and it doesn't stain fabrics. U.S. Army experimenters found that when ticks walked on permethrin-sprayed combat uniforms, they died before they traveled 12 inches. The EPA has not yet approved the product for use by the public, but it is available in at least thirty-one states under special need provisions.

Permanone is manufactured by Fairfield American Corporation in New Jersey, and distributed in the form of an aerosol spray by Coulston International Corporation of Easton, Pennsylvania. The manufacturer warns that the product is for use only on clothing, and not on skin. Lawrence Feller, director of Coulston International, says, "It's aimed at avid sportsmen and people who make their living outdoors. It's not for going on a Saturday afternoon picnic." DEET products are recommended for normal outdoor activities.

How to Remove a Tick

Even with the best precautions, there's still a chance that you'll find a tick on your skin. Don't panic. The first thing to do is to get it off.

Since the tick usually crawls around for a while before it settles down to its meal, you may be able simply to brush it off. But if it is firmly attached, with its mouthparts buried in your skin, getting rid of it is more difficult.

When we first moved to the country, helpful friends and neighbors were free with advice on how to remove ticks. Each had a favorite folk remedy, and over the years we read about others. Most of them didn't work. We thought perhaps we weren't applying the techniques correctly, but according to an experiment conducted by tick physiologist Glen Needham, most of the

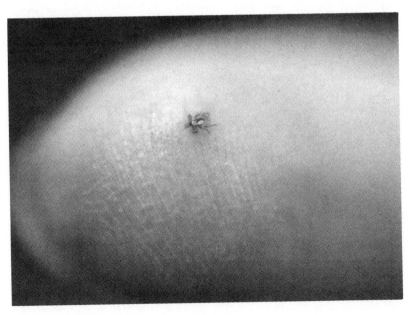

Don't panic if you find a tick on your skin.

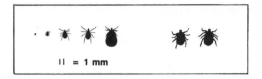

Actual size of deer ticks: *from left*, larva, nymph, adult male and female, and engorged female. Dog ticks are shown on the right.

folk remedies really *don't* work. He tried removing 100 ticks from sheep using all the popular methods like putting Vaseline (petroleum jelly), butter, ointment, rubbing alcohol, kerosene, and gasoline on the tick, placing an extinguished but still hot match or cigarette near the tick, and even coating the tick with ·nail polish. His conclusion: "The best thing to do is just pull the buggers off and not mess with all those other things."

In fact, these other folk remedies can actually cause more damage. Smearing a tick with Vaseline or butter is supposed to force it to dislodge itself because it can't breathe. (The gooey coating closes up the breathing openings in the tick's body.) However, ticks don't breathe very rapidly and can get along with as few as four breaths in an hour—so trying to get it off this way can be a slow process. Meanwhile, the longer the tick stays lodged in the skin the better the chance of its transmitting the disease. Applying nail polish creates a shell that won't allow the tick to leave, even if it wanted to. The idea behind pouring gasoline and kerosene is to kill the tick, but a dead tick is no easier to remove than a live one. Its barbed mouthparts remain locked in place. Placing a hot match near the tick—and, in fact, all the other methods, too—can make the tick nervous, causing it to spit out more fluid and increasing the chances of its transmitting the disease.

Dr. Needham points out that you shouldn't just yank a tick off, however. Squeezing its body may force fluid back into the skin. Twisting or jerking it out may also cause the tick to release fluids, and it can leave the mouthparts in the skin.

The best, and safest method is to carefully grasp the tick as close to the skin as possible, preferably with fine-point tweezers or rounded forceps, which are available in pharmacies or in surgical supply stores. The rounded forceps have been found to work best because they allow you to avoid the bloated blood-filled belly and get as close to the mouthparts as possible. If you have to, you can use your fingers as long as you wear rubber gloves, or place a paper towel between your fingers and the tick. You don't want to touch the tick because the fluid can be transmitted through breaks in the skin. Pull upward slowly but steadily until the tick lets go.

A device called the Tick Solution, based on an invention by a Swedish engineer, is now on the market. The kit contains a specially machined tool that grasps the tick and pulls it out by rotating it. The manufacturer is donating part of the income from sales of the Tick Solution to research on Lyme disease.

If You Have Been Bitten by a Tick

After removing the tick, put it in a jar of alcohol, and write down the date of the bite. Disinfect the area where the tick bite occured with alcohol or Betadine (povidone iodine), and wash your hands thoroughly. Most likely, nothing will happen. Even if the tick was a deer tick, not all of these ticks are infected with Lyme bacteria. In some areas only 2 or 3 percent may be carrying the disease, whereas in other areas up to 90 percent have been found to be infected with Lyme bacteria. Even if a tick is infected, it has to be attached to the skin for a while before the disease can be transmitted. Harvard researchers have established that at least one day is required. If you live near a university involved in tick research, you might contact them and bring in the tick to see if it was a deer tick, and if so, whether or not it was infected with *Borrelia burgdorferi*.

Keep an eye on the place where you were bitten for at least a month. If mouth parts remain in the skin or a rash develops, contact your doctor, and bring the tick with you, if possible.

Other Precautions

Health officials advise that it is best to try to keep wildlife off your property. Don't allow areas to become overgrown. Don't have bird feeders, for birds carry the ticks too. Other animals may also come and eat the seeds. Decreasing wildlife in your backyard decreases the tick population, too.

There are also several products available to help free an area of ticks. The manufacturers of Permanone Tick Repellent make other products that contain permethrin. One is sprayed on shrubbery, or picnic areas. There is also a tick, flea, and lice spray, and an aerosol animal spray that kills fifty-five different kinds of bugs. These products are federally licensed and approved.

Another company, EcoHealth in Boston, Massachusetts, manufactures another permethrin product for getting rid of ticks outside the house. Damminix is sold in the form of cardboard tubes filled with cotton treated with permethrin. These tubes are placed under bushes around the yard. Mice take the cotton to use as a soft lining for their underground nests. While the mice are out looking for food at night, ticks climb aboard. The mice go back to their nests, and the ticks drop off into the cotton and die, while the mice are completely unharmed.

Researchers at Harvard University came up with the idea for Damminix. Their studies demonstrated a dramatic reduction in the numbers of infected ticks when the Permethrin-soaked cotton was used. For best results, Damminix should be put out twice a year: in May to prevent the nymphs from infecting new mice and in July to kill the tick larvae. (According to recent studies by Dr. Thomas Mather, after two years, only 10 percent of the mice on the test area were able to infect ticks with *B. burgdorferi*, compared to nearly all the mice on an untreated area.) The Damminix tubes cost about three to four dollars each. They are placed in a grid formation, 10 yards apart. The treatment isn't cheap, but it can rid a property of ticks at a lower cost than applications of a chemical pesticide like Sevin. Damminix is far safer, too.

Prophylactic Antibiotics

Some people are so worried about catching Lyme disease that whenever they go hiking, or go to a beach where the disease is known to be found, they ask their doctor for antibiotics. When a drug or remedy is taken as a preventive measure, rather than as a cure, its use is referred to as prophylactic. The prophylactic use of antibiotics against Lyme disease is a very controversial issue.

Dr. Raymond Dattwyler of SUNY, Stony Brook, does not believe prophylactic antibiotics are a very good idea. Studies by his

93

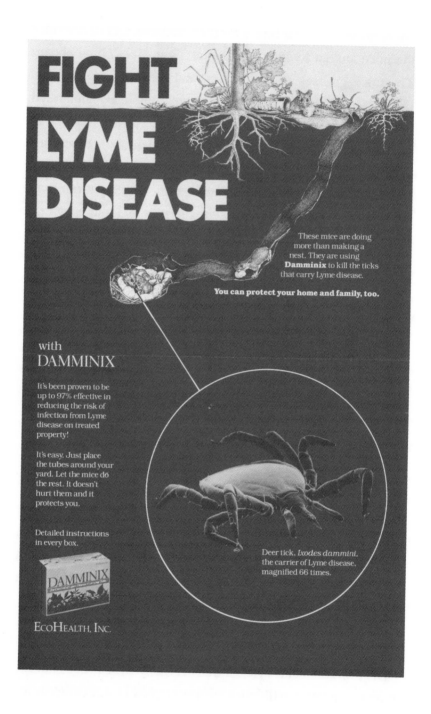

group suggest that people who take antibiotics before visiting an endemic area or before a tick bite have no better chance of avoiding the disease than those who did not take antibiotics.

A New York physician, Dr. Edgar Grunwaldt, points out that the practice of taking antibiotics prophylactically increases the chances of creating strains of bacteria that are resistant to the drugs. "Even treating patients in the absence of symptoms when a tick bite is observed can be a mistake," he says, "because the bite may be from the wrong tick. And the patient may suffer side effects from the antibiotic." He also points out that taking the antibiotics might prevent the buildup of antibodies if an infection did occur, and then blood tests for Lyme disease would not be positive. Such a false negative result might delay effective treatment of the patient.

Dr. Allen Steere found that the average chance of being infected with Lyme disease after an *Ixodes* tick bite is one in thirty. This is about the same as the chance of having adverse side effects from taking antibiotics.

Some doctors, however, like Paul Lavoie in San Francisco, point out that since treatment is not always effective, especially in more advanced cases, and Lyme disease tests are not reliable in determining early cases, "Following a tick bite in a clearly endemic area," he says, "I would treat for two weeks with one of the oral agents."

***

The ultimate form of prevention against Lyme disease will be the development of a vaccination against it. Until effective vaccines are developed, though, the best way to protect yourself is to be tick-smart and take precautions to avoid being bitten by the tiny ticks that carry the Lyme spirochete.

10.
LYME DISEASE AND YOUR PETS

A well adapted parasite does not (usually) kill its host. For if the host always died, the entire host species would soon die out. Then what would the parasite eat? Even making the host ill could eventually lead to the same result, if the illness made the host animal less able to compete in the struggle for life.

Ticks are parasites, which take their nourishment by sucking the blood of animals. The amount of blood in the swollen body of a well-fed tick might seem large in proportion to the tick's normal size, but a healthy host animal can spare it. Each tick feeds only a few times in its entire life, so under normal conditions, these parasites are not likely to bleed their host species into extinction.

In a similar way, the *Borrelia* spirochetes that are parasites on the ticks do not seem to seriously damage their hosts. In the natural cycle, *Ixodes* ticks live on white-footed mice and white-tailed deer, but none of the species seems to be particularly bothered—even when the ticks themselves are infected with Lyme spirochetes. (Of course, it is rather difficult to tell whether wild creatures are feeling well, but the huge numbers of mice in wooded areas and the exploding populations of white-tailed deer suggest that neither species is suffering from any serious health problems.)

Yet parasitic diseases are major health problems, both for

humans and for various animal species. How can that be, if a well-adapted parasite does not damage its host? The problems arise when a parasite transfers to some other host species— one to which it is not so well adapted. That is what we have been seeing with the deer tick. In addition to the two main hosts of its normal life species, *Ixodes dammini* can also feed on more than eighty other kinds of animals.

Rabbits, possums, raccoons, squirrels, chipmunks, voles, and numerous species of birds are among the wild animals to which the deer tick may turn, if its main hosts are not handy. Deer ticks can also infest domestic animals: horses, cattle, and other livestock, as well as pets such as dogs and cats.

Lyme Disease on the Farm

Ralph Janzer, a dairy farmer near Campbellsport, Wisconsin, had an especially costly experience with Lyme disease. Nearly his entire herd of sixty cattle were diagnosed with this ailment. Their joints became so swollen that they cold barely move without severe pain. The cows lost their appetite and, for a while, they were unable to breed.

Lyme disease
can cause
eye problems
in horses.

97

Veterinarians in many parts of the country have become all too familiar with Lyme disease and are quick to suspect it when animals lose weight and suffer from fever, stiff and swollen joints, and general listlessness. In a 1986 study of farms in New Jersey, 60 percent of the horses examined had Lyme antibodies, and almost 20 percent of the foals born that year had arthritis!

The standard treatment for Lyme disease in farm and pet animals is high-dose antibiotic therapy for a full month.

The Threat to Pets

Scott Parry of Norwalk, Connecticut felt as though he was suffering, too, when his three-year-old golden retriever, Toby, came down with Lyme disease. Even after treatment by the local veterinarian, Toby was so crippled he could hardly walk. "It's as if he's old before his time," Parry commented.

Dogs are far more likely to become infected than people—six times as likely, in fact. The number of cases of Lyme disease among dogs has increased more than fourfold in the past six or seven years.

Dogs don't develop a rash when they are bitten by a deer tick, but the test for *Borrelia* antibodies is fairly reliable for them. Usually the disease produces a general listlessness—the dog doesn't seem as lively as it used to, and it sleeps more than usual. Fever, loss of appetite, and an arthritic stiffness and swelling of the joints are also common. Heart ailments may develop and may eventually lead to death.

In the early stages, owners might not realize their pet is ill. They assume that it is just showing the signs of natural

aging. Sometimes the symptoms are so slight, they are not noticeable. A screening program in a veterinary hospital in Westchester County, New York revealed that nearly three quarters of the dogs in the area tested positive for Lyme antibodies. In most cases their owners had not thought the dogs were ill—until the veterinarian treated them with antibiotics. After a few weeks, many of the owners realized their pets seemed much more lively and energetic than they had been for a long time.

Lyme antibody tests are not as reliable for cats, so veterinarians are not sure exactly how common Lyme disease is among cats. But it does seem that they are less likely than dogs to develop the disease. This is probably the result of the fact that cats groom themselves far more than dogs do. Since a tick may wander around a cat for some time before it decides on a place to settle down, it is likely to be licked away before it can do any harm.

Protecting Pets from Lyme Disease

In areas where Lyme disease is endemic, it is practically

impossible to keep outdoor pets completely safe from infection. As they roam outside—even in a well-kept lawn—they may pick up ticks. (One indoor dog developed Lyme disease, even though its owner reported that it never went outside for more than a few minutes, once a day, to urinate and defecate right outside the back door.)

Flea and tick collars are of some help, at least reducing the numbers of ticks the pet may pick up. For dogs, a weekly bath in an antitick solution can provide more protection. Combing with a fine-tooth comb—especially right after the pet has been out for a romp—can remove ticks that are not firmly embedded in the animal's skin. When you find a tick actively feeding on a pet, use the same tick-removal techniques that were described in the last chapter: Grasp the tick firmly (preferably with tweezers or forceps) as close to the head as possible and pull. If the tick's body breaks off and parts of its head still seem to be embedded in the pet's skin, it is advisable to take it to a veterinarian for removal.

All these extra precautions may seem like a lot of bother, but they can be well worth while. You may not only be helping to protect your pet from the miseries of a serious illness, but you may be protecting yourself and your family as well. Ticks carried into the house by a pet may drop off and later crawl onto a human.

If your pet does develop Lyme disease, at least you need not fear that you will catch the illness by handling and caring for it—as long as it is free of ticks. The evidence so far is that Lyme disease is not transmitted by that kind of contact; the bacterium has to be injected into the bloodstream by the bite of a tick.

11.
SOLUTIONS TO THE LYME DISEASE PROBLEM

Lyme disease is still a small problem, as numbers go. (To people suffering from constant headaches, stiff and aching joints, or more serious heart or nervous system disorders, of course, it is a very big problem, indeed!) But another health problem that is worrying Americans these days—AIDS—also started rather recently, in very small numbers. Like AIDS, Lyme disease is spreading at an alarming rate.

Can medical science do anything to stop the spread of Lyme disease? Can we ever eliminate it? Or will we have to give up the pleasures of outdoor living in the summertime? Must we abandon the woods and fields—and even our own back yards— to the tiny eight-legged creatures that are making them more dangerous with each passing year?

So far, we have not made a very large investment in the fight against Lyme disease, compared to other health problems. Already, though, researchers have made great strides in learning about how the disease is transmitted, what it does to the body, and ways it might be controlled.

Breaking the Cycle

Knowledge of the tick's life cycle is an important key to winning the fight against Lyme disease. Fortunately, we do not need to know every detail before we can act. What researchers have already learned suggests some plans of attack.

As we have seen, adult ticks feed and mate on deer. Then they drop off, and the female lays eggs in the grass or woods. The eggs hatch into larvae, which attach themselves to wild mice. The tick larvae grow into nymphs, picking up the *Borrelia* bacterium from the mice while they feed.

It is the nymphs, not the adults, that usually pass the disease to humans.

If we can interrupt this cycle somewhere, we should be able to control Lyme disease.

The Deer Link

Since the deer plays such an important role, serving as a source of food for the adult deer tick, some people have suggested getting rid of the deer—that is, killing them or perhaps moving them to special preserves, away from people.

Will this work?

In the early 1980s an experiment was tried on Great Island, Massachusetts, off the coast of Cape Cod. At the start of the experiment, in 1981, the deer population of the island numbered fifty-four, the tick population was huge, and at least half a dozen cases of Lyme disease were being diagnosed each year among the island's summer residents.

At first, Harvard researcher Andrew Spielman had intended to try to reduce the tick population by treating the deer with insecticides. Unfortunately, it turned out to be harder to catch wild deer than the researcher had expected, and the insecticide treatments didn't work very well on the deer he did catch. (When small containers of insecticide were attached to a deer's ears, for example, the ticks simply crawled away to their host's back or belly and continued their meal.)

The following fall and spring, state game officials began shooting the deer on Great Island. They killed one third of the deer population on the island, but then, in the summer, there was hardly any decrease in the number of tick larvae that hatched out. Killing only part of the deer, commented Connecticut tick researcher John Anderson, has no effect. "The ticks will double up on the deer that are left." As the numbers of deer are decreased further, the ticks turn to other hosts—including humans—and the number of Lyme disease cases goes up!

By 1983, all of the deer on Great Island had been killed, and Lyme disease disappeared among the human residents. Meanwhile, though, a backlash had developed. When the public found out about all the deer being killed, they were outraged. Gen-

Efforts to break the Lyme disease cycle by eliminating deer generate a backlash from Bambi lovers.

erations of Americans had watched the movie, *Bambi*, as children and had special warm feelings toward deer. This "Bambi syndrome," as the media called it, prevented other communities from using the extermination of deer as a solution to the Lyme disease problem.

The Mouse Link

What about another key link in the tick's life cycle: the white-footed mouse? Most people aren't as sentimental about killing mice as they are about killing deer.

Scientists tried to reduce the mouse population by burning the underbrush that provides shelter for them in the woods, but the results were disappointing. Ticks swarmed over the few remaining mice. Soon just about every mouse was infected with the Lyme bacterium. Other ticks, without a natural host to feed on, searched for new sources of blood and used pets and people for their meals. The number of cases of Lyme disease skyrocketed.

The results were better when researchers tried killing the ticks on the mice rather than the mice themselves. The trick was getting the insecticide to the mice. It would not be very practical to try to trap huge numbers of mice and dust them with insecticides. But Harvard researchers Thomas Mather, Andrew Spielman, and Jose Ribeiro came up with an ingenious way to get the mice to treat themselves, as mentioned in Chapter 9.

The Harvard team sprayed fluffy cotton balls with the pesticide permethrin, placed them in cardboard tubes, and spread them in the woods and grassy areas on an 18-acre site. Mice in the area quickly discovered the cotton balls and carried them

Mice collect the Damminix cotton balls for nesting materials; the pesticide kills tick larvae and nymphs without harming the mice.

to their nests. The cotton made such cozy nesting material! While the mice slept in their new cotton nests, the tick larvae and nymphs on them dropped off into the treated cotton. The ticks were killed by the deadly pesticide, but the mice were not harmed. When the Harvard researchers checked mice from the experimental area, thirty-nine out of forty mice they captured were completely free of ticks, and the other mouse had just three ticks. Mice trapped across the road, from an area where no permethrin-treated cotton balls had been placed, were swarming with ticks, averaging twenty each.

The main problem with this approach is cost. The scientists estimated at the time of their experiment, in 1988, that it would cost about $200 to $400 to treat an acre using their method. But the cost is dropping as the new tick-control product, Damminix, is used more widely.

Finding a Parasite for the Parasite

The same Harvard team also explored another way to fight the deer tick. A tiny wasp lays its eggs in tick larvae. The wasp eggs hatch into larvae that feed on the tick nymph, killing it before it can turn into an adult. These wasps have been used to control ticks in France. In the 1920s researchers from Harvard School of Medicine introduced them into Naushon Island, Massachusetts, a region that had been bothered by dog ticks. When the Harvard researchers studied deer ticks on Naushon and nearby Martha's Vineyard in the mid-1980s, they discovered that about 30 percent of the tick nymphs were infested with the wasp parasites. A surprising finding was that none of the nymphs with wasps was infected with *Borrelia* bacteria.

The Harvard scientists speculated that perhaps the mother wasps were picking only uninfected tick larvae in which to lay their eggs. Another possibility might be that the wasp lays her eggs in uninfected larvae, and then the parasites somehow block infection by the bacterium. Even if this does not prove to be true, at least the wasp can help to kill ticks and reduce their numbers. Dr. Thomas Mather and his associates have continued to study the ecology of the wasp and its tick hosts. Dr. Mather is using computer modeling to determine the effects of the wasp parasite on the ticks. He plans to introduce the wasps into a new small island to study the interaction of the two species.

New techniques of biotechnology may help to make such methods of tick control even more effective. Researchers have learned how to transfer genes—the hereditary instructions—from one kind of organism to another. Special "genetically engineered" strains of bacteria are now being used to manufacture a number of proteins—even human proteins such as insulin and growth hormone—from the "blueprints" provided by transferred genes. Cows with specially introduced genes give higher yields of milk. In a laboratory experiment, researchers produced a strain of giant mice as big as rats by introducing human growth hormone genes into mouse embryos. In another experiment, firefly genes were transferred to tobacco plants, and then the plant leaves glowed in the dark.

Some day we may be able to provide people with genes that make tham naturally resistant to microbes such as *Borrelia*. That time is probably far off; genetic engineering experiments with humans have been proceeding very slowly and cautiously. Perhaps a bit sooner, we may be able to engineer more efficient parasites for ticks that can help wipe them out. The parasitic wasp might be a good starting point for such gene tinkering. A bacterium that competes with *Borrelia burgdorferi* (without causing a disease of its own) is another possibility.

Anti-Tick Vaccines

Attacking still another point in the Lyme disease cycle, a group of researchers led by Dr. Glen R. Needham, a tick specialist from Ohio State University, is studying tick saliva. This watery fluid is actually a complicated mixture of chemicals. It contains anticoagulants that keep blood from clotting, so that the tick can continue to sip its blood meal for days at a time without getting its hypostome clogged up. Tick saliva also contains digestive enzymes to break down food materials, as well as a kind of cement that keeps the tick anchored to its host while it is feeding. This cement is a protein, and thus animals can produce antibodies against it.

The discovery of the various proteins in tick cement suggested an intriguing idea. Instead of trying to develop a vaccine to protect people from *Borrelia burgdorferi,* the Lyme disease bacterium, perhaps researchers could develop ways to vaccinate people against the ticks that spread the bacterium. Only animal studies have been conducted so far, but the results are promising.

In one series of experiments, researchers injected partially purified tick cement protein into rabbits, which produced antibodies against the tick protein. When ticks were placed on the immunized rabbits, the ticks tended to fall off the rabbits when they had taken only two-thirds of their usual blood meal. A purer cement protein might stimulate the production of even more effective antibodies. Any reduction of the ticks' feeding time also decreases the chances of their transmitting Lyme disease bacteria.

If scientists could stop the tick from producing saliva in the first place, such a vaccine would provide an even better

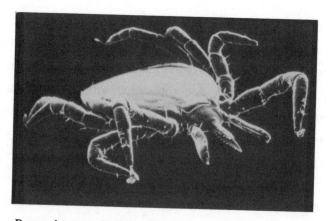

Researchers are looking for ways to fight the deer tick.

defense against Lyme disease. Without the chemicals in its saliva, the tick could not feed effectively; and it is the tick saliva that transmits bacteria to the host. Dr. John Sauer of Oklahoma State University is studying the series of reactions that trigger a tick's secretion of saliva. He hopes to develop a vaccine to block one of these reactions. Such a vaccine could kill ticks or stop them from transmitting disease microbes.

Australian researchers are trying another approach with a distant relative of the *Borrelia* tick. Dr. David Kemp and his colleagues at the CSIRO Division of Tropical Animal Production in Queensland, Australia has developed a vaccine against the cattle tick, *Boophilus microplus*. Using the digestive tracts of fifty thousand ticks, they isolated a tiny amount of tick gut protein. A biotechnology company determined its structure and made a synthetic version, which was then used to vaccinate cattle. When ticks fed on the vaccinated cattle, they took in antibodies along with their blood meal. The antibodies killed ticks by damaging the lining of their gut. In field tests, there was a 91 percent reduction in the number of ticks found on the vaccinated animals.

A similar approach with *Ixodes* ticks might lead to an effective vaccine against them. Anyone who planned to visit tick-infested areas could be vaccinated first and then would not have to worry about contacting Lyme disease.

Some scientist are skeptical about the prospects for this method of disease control. *Ixodes* ticks, they point out, have some powerful defenses against their hosts' immune reactions.

For instance, Dr. Jose M.C. Ribeiro of the Harvard School of Public Health in Boston injected ticks with pilocarpine, a biochemical that makes them drool, just as people do at the smell of food. Dr. Ribeiro collected the tick saliva and found that it contained chemicals that block important parts of the human immune system. This crippling of the immune defenses may explain a puzzling observation. Each time a tick bites a person, it injects a number of foreign proteins. Yet a person can be bitten by ticks again and again without developing effective antibodies against these tick proteins. These tick defenses against our defenses may make it difficult to develop vaccines against them. Or perhaps they may provide another good target for a vaccine attack.

Needed: Better Pesticides

Research approaches such as these may bring solutions to the Lyme disease problem in the future. In the meantime, scientists continue to search for more effective insecticides to replace DEET and other potentially dangerous chemicals now being used. Dr. John F. Carroll, a researcher for the U.S. Department of Agriculture in Beltsville, Maryland, is studying natural plant substances. He has found an oil from an African plant that kills the larvae of the lone star tick and dog tick and repels adult deer ticks. Dr. Carroll is working on determining the structure of the active chemicals in the oil. By changing it in various ways, chemists may be able to make more effective pesticides.

There is another problem with the insecticides we have today. It is not always possible to get them to the right place to kill all the ticks. Researchers from the New Jersey Department of Health discovered this difficulty in an experiment on a 2½ acre plot.

The spraying was performed in the winter, when the trees and bushes were bare. (If sprays are applied in the spring or summer, the chemicals fall mainly on the plant leaves and do not reach the ticks hiding under the leaves or in the ground.) The following spring, there was a substantial decrease in the tick population. But by that fall, there were as many ticks as ever. Researcher Terry L. Schulze of the New Jersey team believes that the spray killed off only adult ticks and did not reach the hibernating larvae. In the spring these immature ticks fed and molted into nymphs, which then proceeded to find a suitable host.

Respraying the same area might kill off this new crop of adults, but tick nymphs from other areas would soon migrate in on mice to build the tick population up again. Only widespread spraying of huge areas might significantly reduce the tick population. But this could cause serious environmental problems. Chemicals that kill ticks also kill insects and spiders—including the ones that do useful things like pollinating flowers and preying on insect pests. "The notion to go out and spray forests for the tick is absolutely insane," says Dr. Durland Fish, an entomologist at New York Medical College.

A Public Concern

Most authorities agree that more public education is probably the most effective measure for now. Connecticut has named May Lyme Disease Awareness Month. In the summer of 1989 the Wisconsin Department of Health mailed out 150,000 brochures explaining how to recognize Lyme disease and prevent getting it. Other states have begun their own education programs.

The states in Lyme disease hot spots are backing their educational programs with money. New York State spends nearly a million dollars each year to support research and educational programs in its battle against Lyme disease. The Federal government is spending several million dollars in the support of research against Lyme disease.

Expenditures will climb in the years ahead. As Paul Etkind, an official from the Massachusetts Public Health Department, says "Lyme disease is second only to AIDS in public interest and concern."

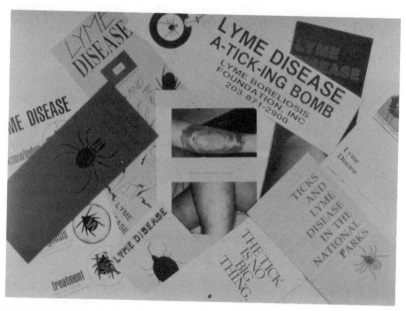

Some educational pamphlets about Lyme disease.

12.
QUESTIONS PEOPLE ASK ABOUT LYME DISEASE

1. What is Lyme disease?

Lyme disease is a bacterial infection that can produce skin rashes, arthritis, heart problems, and neurological disorders.

2. What causes Lyme disease?

Lyme disease is caused by a bacterium spread by the bite of deer ticks and other ixodid tick relatives.

3. What does the deer tick look like?

Deer ticks are much smaller than common dog ticks. The immature nymphs, which are most likely to transmit the disease, are only about the size of a poppy seed. They are a brownish black in color, but after feeding they become more grayish and may swell up to more than three times their size. Adult deer ticks are about the size of a sesame seed. The adult female is a brick red color, with a black shield on her back. The adult male, which is less likely to transmit the disease, is all black. Adult ticks become a blue/black color after feeding and may swell up to the size of a small pea.

4. Where can people get Lyme disease?

Deer ticks can be found in the woods, at beaches, in bushes and brush, tall grass, and even on well-kept lawns. They can also be brought indoors on clothing or in the fur of pets.

5. Are deer ticks found more in some places than others?

By 1989 ixodid ticks had been reported in 43 states in the U.S. and on every continent in the world, except Antartica.

Can you spot the ten ticks lurking in this scene? From educational materials distributed by the Westchester County, New York, Department of Health for a Girl Scouts "Tickbuster" merit badge.

However, most of the cases in the U.S. have been found in certain "hot spot" areas. Six northeastern states: Connecticut, Massachusetts, New Jersey, New York, Pennsylvania, and Rhode Island, along with California, Minnesota, and Wisconsin, account for 95% of all the cases reported in the U.S.

6. How many people have gotten Lyme disease?

Between 1980 and 1989 approximately 21,000 cases of Lyme disease were reported to the Centers for Disease Control (CDC). However, many health officials believe there may actually be as many as 15,000 new cases each year—most unreported.

7. Is Lyme disease spreading?

Many experts believe the deer ticks are increasing the range of their natural habitation. In the 1920s the northern deer tick, for example, was reported only on an island in Massachusetts. By the 1980s this tick was found along the northeastern coast from New Hampshire to Virginia, and as far inland as Pennsylvania and Maryland. With the spread of the ticks, Lyme disease is also spreading. In 1980, when the CDC first began monitoring Lyme disease cases, the disease was reported in only 11 states. By 1989 43 states had reported cases of Lyme disease.

8. When are people most likely to be bitten by deer ticks?

In the northeast, deer ticks normally feed from April to November. Most bites occur in June and July, when the nymphs are most likely to feed. October and November are another lesser peak, when adult females feed to produce the 2500 eggs they will lay in the spring. In milder weather and in warmer areas around the country, ticks may bite at any time of year.

9. How can I protect myself from Lyme disease?

If you are going hiking or camping or visiting a place ticks are known to be abundant, be tick-smart. Take precautions to keep ticks away. When walking or hiking, stay near the center of paths and trails. Wear light-colored clothing so you can see if ticks climb aboard. Wear closed shoes, long pants, and long-sleeved shirts whenever possible. Tuck pant bottoms into socks or boots, and shirt into pants. check your clothes often and brush off any dark spots. Some experts suggest using insect or tick repellents that contain DEET on clothes at tick entrance spots like shoes, socks, pant and sleeve cuffs. Wash clothes when you get home, take a shower to remove unattached ticks, and check yourself completely for ticks—on the scalp, in and behind the ears, neck, back, underarms, groin area, back of the knees, and lower legs.

10. What can I do if I live in a Lyme disease "hot spot" area?

If you live in a place known to be a deer tick problem area, take precautions against ticks daily, especially in the summer

Warning

TICKS MAY BE FOUND IN THIS AREA

To avoid tick bites:

Wear light colored clothing and tuck trouser cuffs in socks

Apply insect repellent to clothing below the waist

Examine clothing and skin frequently for ticks

Carefully remove attached ticks immediately

Actual size of an immature tick is •

For more information call (914) 285-LYME

Andrew P. O'Rourke, County Executive
Anita S. Curran, M.D., M.P.H, Commissioner, Dept. of Health

Westchester County

when the most time is spent outdoors. Check for ticks often. Don't walk pets in woods, thick brush, or tall grass. Shower every day. Keep wildlife off your property to reduce ticks. Don't have bird feeders or leave food out for squirrels. Experts suggest pesticide sprays (check with your local health department about risks) or products like Damminix to reduce tick populations.

11. What do I do if I'm bitten by a tick?

If you're bitten by a tick, don't panic. Most biting ticks are dog ticks, not deer ticks, and even if it is a deer tick the tick must feed for a while before the disease can be transmitted. Experts advise removing the tick as soon as possible using tweezers or forceps. Grasp the tick as close to the skin as possible, avoiding the bloated abdomen. Pull firmly and steadily without twisting or jerking until the tick lets go. Apply antiseptic, put the tick in a jar of alcohol, and wash hands thoroughly. If the mouthparts remain in your skin, see a doctor. Note the date and location of the bite and keep an eye on it for at least a month. If you develop symptoms, consult a doctor.

12. What are Lyme disease symptoms?

Most people who are bitten by a deer tick never notice they have been bitten. Lyme disease symptoms can appear anywhere from days to years after being bitten by an infected tick, and the symptoms vary greatly.

Many people who develop Lyme disease get a bull's-eye rash, with a clear center area. But not everyone gets the rash. Flu-like symptoms are also common, including fever, headache, fatigue, stiff neck, and joint or muscle pain. Weeks or months later, more severe symptoms involving the heart or nervous system may appear, including meningitis, encephalitis or facial palsy. Severe arthritis can also develop months or years after a bite.

13. How is Lyme disease diagnosed?

Current Lyme disease blood tests usually will not detect the disease until at least 3 or 4 weeks after being bitten. Many health officials suggest that all bull's-eye rashes in patients in endemic areas (where ticks are firmly established) be treated as Lyme disease, even with a negative blood test.

14. How is Lyme disease treated?

Most patients who are treated early with oral antibiotics recover completely (although symptoms may persist for months in some cases). In later stages hospitalization may be necessary, and antibiotics may need to be administered by injection (intravenously). Because not all patients respond to antibiotic treatments when the disease has become severe, health experts stress the need to begin treatment as soon as possible.

Once Lyme disease is treated and cured, blood tests may still come out positive for months afterwards.

15. Can Lyme disease infect pets?

Dogs are even more likely to contract Lyme disease than people, because they are typically outside more. Cats don't seem to be infected as often but can just as easily carry the ticks inside your home. Tick collars should be worn at all times, and tick powders, sprays, or baths might be recommended by your veterinarian. Pets should be brushed with a fine-toothed brush daily, and checked regularly for ticks. Because pets can bring ticks inside, experts recommend they not be allowed on couches, or to sleep in bed with humans. Symptoms of pets with Lyme disease include sluggishness, loss of appetite, and swollen joints.

16. Is it possible to get Lyme disease without getting bitten

by a tick? From a mosquito? By kissing someone? Through a blood transfusion? Using someone's toothbrush, or razor, or towel?

Researchers are not sure whether or not the Lyme disease bacteria can be transmitted any other way than by a tick bite. Some insist not, but some scientists believe it can be transmitted through saliva and urine. Some think that transmission through blood transfusions—as in AIDS cases—may also be possible. No cases of transmission by sharing a toothbrush or razor have been reported, but there is a possibility it could happen if infected blood is passed to someone with a cut that allows bacteria to get inside the body. It is not likely that Lyme disease could be transferred by sharing towels, swimming in the same pool as someone who has it, or other forms of casual contact. Lyme disease also does not seem to be spread by sexual activity. Researchers believe that mosquitoes do not transmit Lyme disease, although the *Borrelia* bacteria have been found in these insects. A mosquito feeds for a very short time, and hours or days may be needed for the disease to be transmitted through a tick.

15. What else can be done about Lyme disease?

Write your senators, congressmen, local and state government officials voicing your concern about Lyme disease. This is a growing problem that has only recently become known to the general public, and yet one that affects a growing number of people. More funds are desperately needed by researchers to help devise better methods to test for the disease, more effective ways to treat it, and ultimately to develop a vaccine that will protect people from infection.

FOR FURTHER INFORMATION

Suggested Reading

Altman, Lawrence K., "Medical Science Steps Up its Assault On Lyme Disease," *New York Times,* July 4, 1989. pp. C15+.

Altman, Lawrence K., "Lyme Disease From a Transfusion? It's Unlikely, but Experts Are Wary," *New York Times,* July 17, 1989, p. C3.

Benzaia, Diana, "Is It Lyme Disease?" *Health,* June 1989, pp. 72-75.

Benzaia, Diana, *Protect Yourself From Lyme Disease,* Dell Publishing, New York, 1989.

Folkenberg, Judy, "Tick Time: How To Protect Dogs From Lyme Disease," *American Health,* April 1990, p 110.

Habicht, Gail S, et al., "Lyme Disease," *Scientific American,* July 1987, pp. 78-83.

Hixson, Joseph R., "Harvard Enlisting Mice in War on Lyme Disease," *Medical Tribune,* October 20, 1988, p 3.

Kruschhwitz, Kate, "TickTickTickTickTick...Advances in Diagnosis and Prevention Offer Hope in the Race to Defuse Lyme-Disease Explosion," *Equus,* June 1989, pp 140-141.

Makover, Michael E., M.D., "Tick, Tick, Tick," *New York,* May 22, 1989, pp. 77-78.

New York Medical College, "Special Issue--Lyme Disease," *Images,* Fall/Winter 1989.

Rothschild, Richard D., "The Lyme Ticks are Coming!" *American Health,* April 1990, pp. 11-12.

Seligmann, Jean, et al., "Tiny Tick, Big Worry," *Newsweek,* May 22, 1989, pp. 66-72.

Schmitz, Anthony, "After the Bite," *Hippocrates,* May/June 1989, pp. 78-84.

Sobel, Dava, "Pesticides Studied in the Fight Against Lyme Disease," *The New York Times,* April 18, 1989, p C4.

Thomas, Patricia, "Mice Enlisted to Fight Lyme Disease," *Medical World News,* October 10, 1988, p 88.

"Watch Out for the Tick Attack," *Consumer Reports,* June 1988, pp. 382-385.

Wickelgren Ingrid, "At the Drop of a Tick," *Science News,* March 25, 1989, pp. 184-187.

For More Information, contact:

1) Your State or county Health Department epidemiology section.

2) National Lyme Borreliosis Foundation
   Box 462
   Tolland, CT 06084   (203) 871-2900

3) Local Arthritis Foundation chapters (some, like the New York chapter, sponsor meetings for Lyme patients)

   Arthritis Foundation
   P. O. Box 19000
   Atlanta, GA 30326   (404) 872-7100

4) One of the Major University centers actively involved in Lyme disease research and treatment:

   Harvard School of Public Health
   Boston, MA 02115
   (617) 432-1000

   Mayo Clinic
   Rochester, MN 55905
   (507) 284-2111

   University of Medicine &
   Dentistry of New Jersey
   One Robert Wood Johnson Place
   New Brunswick, NJ 08901
   (201) 937-7600

   University of Minnesota
   Medical School
   St. Paul, MN 55455
   (612) 625-1155

   New York Medical College
   Center for the Study and
   Treatment of Lyme Disease
   Valhalla, NY 10595
   (914) 285-1700

   State University of New
   York at Stony Brook
   School of Medicine
   Stony Brook, NY 11794
   (516) 444-3808

   Tufts University—New
   England Medical Center
   750 Washington St.
   Boston, MA 02111
   (617) 956-5789

   Yale University
   School of Medicine
   New Haven, CT 06510
   (203) 785-2453

5) U.S. Centers for Disease Control
   Division of Vector Borne
   Infectious Diseases
   Fort Collins, CO 80522
   (303) 221-6400

6) National Institute of Allergy
   & Infectious Disease (NIAID)
   Building 31, Room 7A-32
   9000 Rockville Pike
   Bethesda, MD 20891
   (301) 496-5717

7) NIAMS
   Bldg 31, Room 4C05
   9000 Rockville Pike
   Bethesda, MD 20891

8) Department of Health and
   Human Services
   Rocky Mountain Laboratory
   Hamilton, MT 59840

9) EcoHealth (manufacturer of Damminix)
   33 Mount Vernon Street
   Boston, MA 02100
   (800) 234-TICK

10) A brochure prepared by Pfizer is available from your state or county
    Health Department, or from:
    Pfizer Central Research
    Groton, CT 06340

11) Westchester County Health Department has pamphlets and posters
    available:
    Westchester County Dept of Health
    County Office Bldg 2
    112 E Post Rd
    White Plains, NY 10601
    (914) 285-LYME

GLOSSARY

antibody - a protein that recognizes and attacks specific antigens.

antigen - a foreign substance that simulates the production of specific antibodies.

arachnid - one of a group of eight-legged animals including spiders and ticks.

arthralgia - pain in the joints.

arthritis - disorder characterized by inflammation and degenerative changes in the joints.

arthropods - a group of animals including insects and arachnids.

autoimmune disease - disorder resulting from attack of the immune system on the body's own tissues.

B cells - lymphocytes that produce antibodies.

Bell's palsy - a paralysis of facial muscles, usually on one side.

Borrelia burgdorferi - the Lyme Disease spirochete.

borreliosis - infection with *Borrelia.*

chronic - long-lasting.

DEET - N,N-diethyl-meta-toluamide, a tick repellent.

ELISA - enzyme-linked immunosorbent assay, a type of test for Lyme disease antibodies.

endemic area - region where a disease is known to be present.

erythema chronicum migrans (ECM) - the bull's eye rash typical of Lyme disease.

hypostome - the tick's barbed mouth.

IFA - immunofluorescence assays, a type of test for Lyme disease antibodies.

inflammation - a body defense reaction involving fever and swelling of tissues with fluid.

interleukin-1 (IL-1) - a body chemical that stimulates inflammation.

intravenous injection - injection into a vein.

Ixodes dammini - the deer tick.

Jarisch-Herxheimer reaction - a temporary worsening of symptoms after antibiotic treatment.

larva - in tick development, the immature form that hatches from the egg.

lipopolysaccharide (LPS) - a complex chemical found in the bacterial cell wall, consisting of fat and sugar portions.

lymphocytes - white blood cells involved in immune defenses.

nymph - in tick development, an immature stage between the larva and the adult.

oral drug - a drug taken by mouth.

palps - "feelers"—sense organs on a tick's head.

parasite - an organism that feeds on a living host.

PCR - polymerase chain reaction, a technique used in research to detect DNA of *Borrelia burgdorferi.*

permethrin - a synthetic insecticide that kills ticks.

phagocyte - a type of white blood cell that engulfs and eats invading microbes.

spirochete - a corkscrew-shaped bacterium.

T cells - a group of lymphocytes whose functions include distinguishing between "self" and "foreign" chemicals, helping or suppressing B cells, and attacking invading microbes or cancer cells.

vector - an animal or insect that carries and spreads a disease.

INDEX

ABOUT THE AUTHORS:

DR. ALVIN SILVERSTEIN is a professor of biology at the College of Staten Island of the City University of New York.

VIRGINIA SILVERSTEIN is a translator of Russian scientific literature.

This husband-and-wife team has collaborated on more than eighty published books. The Silversteins live in rural New Jersey, in an old stone house on a partly wooded hill, where the deer come up to the house to munch on their azaleas and yews.

ROBERT SILVERSTEIN, a graduate of Rutgers University with a major in Communications, joined his parents' writing team in 1988 and has already coauthored six books with them. He lives with his wife, Linda, and baby daughter, Emily, in a small New Jersey town not far from the farm where he spent his teen years.